THE LIFE OF PAUL

A SERVANT OF
JESUS CHRIST

THE LIFE OF PAUL

F. B. MEYER

Edited for Today's Reader by
LANCE WUBBELS

Emerald
Books

P.O. Box 635
Lynnwood, Washington 98046

Scripture quotations are taken from the King James Version of the Bible.

The Life of Paul

Copyright © 1995
Lance C. Wubbels

ISBN 1-883002-22-2

Published by Emerald Books
P.O. Box 635
Lynnwood, Washington 98046

Printed in the United States of America.

CONTENTS

About The Editor

LANCE WUBBELS, the Managing Editor of Bethany House Publishers, taught biblical studies courses at Bethany College of Missions for many years. he is also the author of *The Gentle Hills* fiction series and a heartwarming short novel, *One Small Miracle*, with Bethany House.

As the compiler and editor of the Charles Spurgeon and F.B. Meyer Christian Living Classic books, Wubbels' desire is to present these classic writings in a way that will appeal to a wide audience of readers and allow their timeless messages to be as relevant today as the day they were penned. The writings of both Spurgeon and Meyer are filled with practical insight that will enrich believers' lives.

INTRODUCTION

For over a century, the writings of F.B. Meyer have provided Christians with a treasure trove of lasting value, affirming the truths of the gospel for every age. Crowning a life of worldwide ministry by voice and pen, Meyer's books reflect a depth of spiritual experience and singlemindedness of vision that one rarely finds in contemporary writing. It is for this reason that Lance Wubbels has chosen to edit and update this remarkable biography of one of God's greatest biblical saints.

F.B. Meyer wrote twelve portraits of the giants of the Old and New Testaments. These detailed, inspirational biographies are filled with insight, challenge, and comfort. It is comforting to find that these great figures were not so different from ourselves—sometimes weak, indifferent, willful. Yet they had their moments of faith, humility, and courage, and God was able to use these for His greater purposes. God's faithfulness, which not only accepts but transforms such inconsistency, calls us to more effective Christian living.

It cannot be stressed enough that these are thoroughly biblical portraits. It is essential that the scripture listed at the beginning of each chapter be read first. Meyer's wrote the chapter with it firmly in his mind that the reader would have his Bible opened to that scripture and be completely familiar with its context. Attempting to read the chapter without studying the listed scripture will leave the reader in the dark at some points. The editor gives his strongest recommendation that you first read the scripture and then follow along as Meyer develops his thoughts based upon the biblical text.

You are invited to read these powerful chapters as you would listen to a trusted and skilled pastor. There is nothing speculative about Meyer's teaching. He will meet you where you live in an understandable manner that inspires and challenges, and you will not be disappointed. Life-changing messages await your reading.

Careful editing has helped to sharpen the focus of these messages and update the language while retaining the authentic and timeless flavor they undoubtedly bring.

1

PREVENIENT GRACE

A city throned upon the height behold,
Wherein no foot of man as yet has trod;
The City of man's Life fulfilled in God—
Bathed all in light, with open gates of gold.

Phillips Brooks

*C*ontrary to what we usually think, the source of a stream must be sought not where it arises in some green pasture among the hills, making a tiny pool of clear water where the mountain sheep come down to drink, but in the mighty sea that is drawn upward in evaporation or in the clouds that condense against the close slopes of the hills. So with the life of God within us. In its earlier stages, we are apt to suppose it originated in our will and choice, and we return to our Father's house. But as we review it from the eminence of the years, we discover that we chose because we were chosen, that we loved because we were first loved, that we left the sepulcher of our selfishness and the shroud of death because the Son of God flung His majestic word into the sepulchral vault, crying, "Come forth!" All mature godliness extols the grace

9

of God—the unmerited love that every believer thinks was magnified most abundantly in his own case. "But by the grace of God I am what I am" (1 Cor. 15:10) is a confession made by every man as he reaches the crest of the hill and looks back on the cities of the plain from which he has escaped.

Paul is very emphatic in his acknowledgement of this prevenient grace. He loves to trace back all the good that was in his heart and life to a love that was set on him before the mountains were brought forth, even before God had formed the earth and the world. In the silence of eternity, God's delights had already been with Paul as a son of man.

FOREKNOWN

"Known unto God," said the solemn James at the Jerusalem Council, "are all his works from the beginning of the world" (Acts 15:18). And if His works were foreknown, how much more His saints! Again the evangelist tells us that Jesus knew from the beginning who they were who believed not and who would betray Him. Surely, then, He must have known from the beginning who the believers were and who would become His devoted lovers and apostles. Before time began, it was known in heaven who would be attracted by the love of the cross to trust, love, and obey; who would be drawn to the dying and risen Son of God; who would have eternal affinity with Him in death and resurrection. Of these it is said, "For whom he did foreknow, he also did predestinate to be conformed to the image of his Son, that he might be the firstborn among many brethren" (Rom. 8:29).

It is not a complete solution of the mystery of predestination—and only removes it one stage further back—yet the suggestion casts a gleaming torchlight into the darkness of the impenetrable abyss when we are told that God included in the eternal purposes of life all those whom He foresaw would be attracted to an indissoluble union of faith and life with His Son. All who come to Jesus show that they were included in the Father's gift to His Son. The Father gave Him all those who in the fullness of times should come. But why some have an affinity with the Man of the cross and not others, why some come and others stay away, why some sheep hear the Shepherd's voice and follow while others persist in straying, is one of those secrets that are not revealed as yet to the children of men.

But as the eye of omniscient love glanced down the ages, it must have lighted with peculiar pleasure on the eager, devoted soul of Paul. God foreknew and predestinated him. The divine purpose, foreseeing Paul's capacity for the best, selected him for it and it for him. And there is a gleam of holy rapture on Paul's face when, reviewing the process of those eternal movements of love from his Roman prison, he writes, "Blessed be the God and Father of our Lord Jesus Christ, who hath blessed us with all spiritual blessings in heavenly places in Christ: According as he hath chosen us in him before the foundation of the world" (Eph. 1:3-4).

CREATED IN CHRIST JESUS UNTO GOOD WORKS

Paul has been showing the place of works in the gospel scheme, insisting with unusual emphasis and sharpness of outline that neither our salvation nor our faith is matter for boasting. "It is the gift of God: not of works," he cries (Eph. 2:8-9), and then he proceeds to the magnificent assertion, "For we are his workmanship, created in Christ Jesus unto good works, which God hath before ordained that we should walk in them" (Eph. 2:10).

The Greek word translated *workmanship* is *poem*. We are God's poem. As we review our life after the passing of years—except where we have willfully violated the obvious intention of our Creator—we shall perceive that there has been an underlying plan and design, the development of which has proceeded in ever-widening circles. "I girded thee, though thou hast not known me" (Isa. 45:5) is as true of our life as of Cyrus, who was raised up to be the destroyer of Babylon and the liberator of the people of God. God has a distinct thought in each human life. He creates with a purpose. As a great poet may adopt various kinds of rhythm and measure such as may suit his design, but has nevertheless a purpose in each poem that issues from his creative fancy, so God means something as He sends each life forth from the silence of eternity. If we do not hinder God, He superintends the embodiment of that design, making our entire life, from the cradle to the grave, a symmetrical and homogeneous poem, dominated by one thought though worked out with an infinite variety of illustration and detail.

In a poem, the expression is adapted to the design. A rugged strain befits strong and terse thinking, while more flowing and sweet measures are better adapted to tender and plaintive musings. Possibly we can thus account for the differences that characterize human lives. Yonder is the fragment of a great epic, there the lyric or dramatic, here the sonnet or elegy. Your life is smooth and flowing, or broken over stones of sorrow, or headlong in its impetuosity because God's thought must be mated to the meter most suited for its expression. Paul's career reminds us of the *Odyssey,* the *Iliad,* the *Paradise Lost,* or the mighty conception of Dante. It is oceanlike in depth, variety, and change. As in an oratorio, so here the storehouse of expression is ransacked to convey the deep and varied transition of the Creator's thought, emotion, and passion.

The poet's art demands that no detail of description or narrative in the earlier lines should be fruitless or redundant. To allow a canvas to be covered by figures or objects that do not lead to the main intention of a picture is in the highest degree reprehensible. Watch well the earlier chapters of a great tale, and you will notice that the details and descriptions of every paragraph prepare for the ultimate unfolding of the story, leading up to the climax to which the closing pages hurry.

So in human life. God knows the works that are prepared that we should walk in them. And as He has created them for us, so has He created us for them, in Christ Jesus. The year of our birth, the place and scenes of early childhood, our parentage and education, the influences that have shaped us—whether of books or art or the conditions of daily toil—have been planned with an unerring wisdom and predisposition, that through us might be made known unto the principalities and powers in the heavenly places "the manifold wisdom of God, according to the eternal purpose which he purposed in Christ Jesus our Lord: in whom we have boldness and access with confidence by the faith of him" (Eph.3:10–12).

It was thus a matter of constant pleasure to the apostle Paul that he did not have to cut or carve his way but simply had to discover the track that God had prepared for his steps from of old. And when he found it, it not only would be consistent with his place in the mystical Body of Christ but also would be the very pathway for which his character and gifts were most adapted.

RAISED IN CHRIST'S RESURRECTION

Paul's education differed widely from that of his fellow apostles, who had grown up with Christ. It is likely that the Master was familiar with many of them before He called them. No one has traveled down from the highland village of Nazareth to the blue waters of Galilee without realizing how easy and constant the fellowship must have been during those thirty silent years. The other apostles, therefore, grew gradually into the mysteries of His death and resurrection. They knew Jesus the man before they recognized Christ the Messiah. From the Jordan valley they had been ascending the hill of the Lord and were therefore less amazed when the sharp, steep spur of Calvary suddenly confronted them, surmounted by the peaks of resurrection and ascension rising in peerless beauty beyond.

To Paul, on the other hand, the first vision of Jesus was in His risen glory. Paul knew perfectly, for it was common talk when he was a resident in Jerusalem, that Jesus had been crucified under Pontius Pilate. But now he beheld Him risen, living, speaking, His face shining with light above the brightness of the sun. It was a spectacle that could never be erased from his memory. Besides answering all his difficulties, it gave an aspect to his faith that he never lost. The "yea rather, that is risen again" of Romans 8:34 is very significant. Paul had to think his way back from the ascension and resurrection glory to Calvary, Gethsemane, the human life, and the faraway scenes of the Lord's nativity and early years.

But more than this, Paul had a very vivid belief in the identification of all who believe with the risen Lord, and that from the moment of His resurrection. Paul held and taught that all the members of the mystical body shared in the experiences and exploits of their Head. What happened to Jesus Christ happened to them also, and to each of them. There was no single believer, therefore, who could not avow as his own all that had befallen Jesus, though at the time he might have been dead in his trespasses and sins or had not even yet been born.

The apostle never allowed his views of personal union with the Savior to clash with his presentation of the unique character of that death, by virtue of which He did for men what no one man, nor all men together, could have done. Paul always taught that the death on the cross was a propitiating sacrifice for the sins of the whole world—a sacrifice that stands alone in its sublime and unapproachable glory. But he loved to dwell on that other and secondary aspect of the Savior's death by virtue of which, in the divine intention, all who believe are reckoned one with Him in his death, resurrection, and ascension into the heavenlies.

In one memorable text, Paul connects these two aspects of the cross: "who loved me, and gave himself *for* me" is bound by a golden link to the words "I am crucified *with* Christ" (Gal. 2:20). He is always clear in saying, "While we were yet sinners, Christ died for us.... we were reconciled to God by the death of his Son" (Rom. 5:8, 10). But he is as clear and emphatic in saying, "Even when we were dead in sins, [God] hath quickened us together with Christ, (by grace ye are saved;) and [God] hath raised us up together, and made us sit together in heavenly places in Christ Jesus" (Eph. 2:5-6). "That one died for all" (2 Cor. 5:14) was an undoubted article in his creed; but this was another: "That our old man is crucified with him, that the body of sin might be destroyed, that henceforth we should not serve sin" (Rom. 6:6). Paul loved to reckon that he had died with Christ and to claim that he should daily receive the power of His risen life. He longed to know Jesus Christ and the power of His resurrection, being quite prepared to taste the fellowship of His sufferings and to become conformed unto His death if only he might day by day attain unto the resurrection of the dead (Phil. 3:10-11).

This conception of Paul's union with Christ in death and resurrection underlies the whole tenor of his appeals to a holy and consecrated life: "If ye then be risen with Christ, seek those things which are above.... For ye are dead, and your life is hid with Christ in God. When Christ, who is our life, shall appear" (Col. 3:1-4).

It was a radiant vision, and one of which the apostle never wearied. It was attributable to nothing less than the great love with which God had loved him when he was a blasphemer and a persecutor and injurious, living, as he confesses he did, in the lusts of his flesh, doing the desires of the flesh and of the mind, and being by nature a child of wrath even as the rest (Eph. 2:3). For us, too, that vision waits; and in battling against the lusts of the flesh, the fascinations of the world, and the power of the devil, there is no position more filled with the certainty of victory than that of our resurrection standing and privilege. When the world would cast the spell of its flatteries over you, dare to answer the challenge by the assertion that it has no further jurisdiction over you, since you have passed from its territory and control by virtue of your union with Him who, in that He died, died unto sin once and, in that He lives, lives to God.

Get up into the high mountains, believing children of God, and view the everlasting love of your Father toward you in Jesus! Recount all that that love has brought for you before you had any being! Is He likely to drop you now because of any unworthiness He perceives? Can anything appear in us that was not anticipated by the One who before taking us for His own possession sat down and counted the cost? Is there not comfort in knowing that your vessel is caught by a current that emanated from the purpose of Him who works all things after the counsel of His own will and is bearing you toward his heart? "O the depth of the riches both of the wisdom and knowledge of God! how unsearchable are his judgments, and his ways past finding out!... For of him, and through him, and to him, are all things: to whom be glory for ever. Amen" (Rom. 11:33, 36).

2

Philippians 3:1–11

WHEN I
WAS A CHILD

*I was bred
In the great city, pent mid cloisters dim,
And saw naught lovely save the sky and stars.*

Coleridge

Not far from the easternmost bay of the Mediterranean, in the midst of a rich and luxuriant plain, stood Tarsus, "no mean city" (Acts 21:39), as one of its greatest sons tells us, but at the time a thriving emporium of trade and a focus of intellectual and religious activity. On the northern edge of the plain rose the mighty Taurus mountains, with their peaks of eternal snow, feeding with perpetual freshness and fullness the river Cydnus, which, after pouring over a cataract of considerable size, passed through the midst of the town and so to the sea. During the last part of its course it was navigable by the largest vessels, bringing the treasures of East and West to the wharves that lined either bank. Here were piled merchandise and commodities of every kind, brought to exchange for the cloth of goat hair for which the town was famous and which was furnished by the flocks of goats that browsed on the lower slopes of the Taurus, tended by the hardy mountaineers. Tarsus also received the trade that poured through the Cilician Gates—a famous pass through the mountains, leading upward from the coast to Central Asia Minor, to Phrygia and Lycaonia on one side and to Cappadocia on the other.

In the Jewish quarter of this thriving city at the beginning of this era (perhaps about A.D. 4, while Jesus was still a young boy), a child was born who by his life and words was destined to make it famous for all time and to give a new inspiration to men's spiritual convictions. At his circumcision, he probably received a double name—that of Saul for his family and that of Paul for the world of trade and municipal life.

The stamp of the great city left an indelible impression on the growing lad, and in this his early years were widely different from his Master's. Jesus was nurtured in a highland village, loved to teach on the hillside, and gathered His illustrations from the field of nature. Paul was reared amid the busy streets and crowded bazaars of Tarsus, thronged with merchants, students, and sailors from all parts of the world. Unconsciously, as the lad grew, Paul was being prepared to understand human life under every aspect and to become familiar with the thoughts and habits of the store, the camp, the arena, the temple. He became a man to whom nothing that touched human life was foreign. He loved the stir of city life and drew his metaphors from its strongest interests.

He came of pure Hebrew stock. "An Hebrew of *(sprung from)* the Hebrews" (Phil. 3:5). On both sides, his genealogy was pure. There was no Gentile admixture in his blood or in his descent. His father must have been a man of considerable position, or he would not have possessed the coveted birthright of Roman citizenship. Though living away from Palestine, he was not a Hellenist Jew and was distinctly Hebrew as any who dwelt in the Holy City herself. Perhaps Paul's father was given to sternness with his children, or it might not have occurred to Paul to warn the Ephesian fathers against provoking their children to wrath lest they should become discouraged. His mother, too, though we have no precise knowledge of her, must have been imbued with those lofty ideas of which we catch a trace in the mothers of Samuel, John the Baptist, and Jesus. Perhaps she died in his early childhood, or Paul would not in later years have so lovingly turned to the mother of Rufus for motherhood (Rom. 16:13).

The Hebrew tongue was probably the ordinary speech of their home. This may in a measure account for the apostle's intimate acquaintance with the Hebrew Scriptures, which Paul so often quotes. It was in Hebrew that Jesus spoke to Paul on the road to Damascus and in Hebrew that Paul addressed the crowds from the steps of the castle. To Paul, Jerusalem was greater than Athens or Rome, and Abraham, David, and Isaiah, greater than the heroes of the *Iliad*. Paul counted it no small thing to have as ancestors those holy patriarchs and prophets who had followed God from Ur, wrestled with the angel at the Jabbok, and spoken to God at Horeb face to face. Paul's pulse beat quick as he remembered that he belonged to the chosen race, God's firstborn, to whom were given the adoption, the glory, the covenants, the giving of the law, the service of God, and the promises. However much nobility and wealth were flaunted before his eyes, Paul held himself to have nobility born of a nobler ancestry, to belong to a higher aristocracy. From his tribe had sprung the first king of Israel, whose name he was proud to bear.

His early education was very religious. "As touching the law, a Pharisee" (Phil. 3:5). In our day, the word *Pharisee* is a synonym for religious pride and hypocrisy, but we must never forget that in those old Jewish days, the Pharisee represented some of the noblest traditions of the Hebrew people. Amid the prevailing indifference, the Pharisees stood for a strict religious life. As against the skepticism of the Sadducees, who believed in neither spirit nor unseen world, the Pharisees held to the resurrection of the dead and the life of the world to come. Amid the lax morals of the time that infected Jerusalem almost as much as they did Rome, the Pharisee was austere in his ideals and holy in life. The texts on his phylacteries at least evidenced his devotion to Scripture; the tithing of mint, cummin, and anise at least proved the scrupulosity of his obedience to the law; his prayers might be a showy display, but they were conspicuous evidence of his belief in the unseen.

Such was the father of the future apostle. His early home was dominated by these austere and strong religious ideals, and the boy imbibed them. According to the strictest sect of his religion, Paul lived a Pharisee. He was proud that at the earliest possible moment he had been initiated into the rites and privileges of his religion, being "circumcised the eighth day" (Phil. 3:5). As he heard of proselytes entering the covenant of his fathers in mature life, he congratulated himself that as a child he had been admitted into covenant relationship with God.

He was blameless in outward life. As "touching the righteousness which is in the law," so far as outward observances went, Paul was "blameless" (Phil. 3:6). There was no precept in the moral or ceremonial law that he would consciously disregard. And though the rabbis had built upon the Law of Moses an immense superstructure of ethical comments and minute injunctions, Paul bravely set himself to master them. He would hold it a crime to enter into the house of a Gentile, and on leaving the market or street, he would carefully wash his hands of any defilement contracted through touching what had been handled by the uncircumcised. He often thanked God that he was not as other men. He was taught to fast twice in the week and give tithes of all he possessed. He would observe the Sabbath and festivals with punctilious and extreme care. "Men and brethren," Paul said on one occasion, "I have lived in all good conscience before God until this day" (Acts 23:1).

The ardent soul of the young Pharisee was bent on standing in the front rank of saints. Early in life, Paul had made up his mind to win the prize of God's favor. He could imagine nothing more desirable than this. When, therefore, in answer to his inquiry of the recognized religious teachers, he learned that absolute obedience to the words of the rabbis was the only method of achieving the object on which his heart was set, he determined with unremitting devotion to scale the perilous heights and tread the glacier slopes. Perhaps he encountered disappointment from the first. Possibly the cry "O wretched man that I am!" (Rom. 7:24) began to formulate itself long before he became a Christian. Though outwardly his conduct was exemplary, his soul may have been torn by mortal strife. Often he saw and approved the better and did the worse; often he lamented the weakness of his motives and the weakness of his will. Conscious of shortcomings that no other eye discerned, Paul yearned for power to spend one absolutely holy day, which, the rabbis taught, if lived by any one Israelite, would secure the immediate advent of the Messiah.

His nature must have been warmhearted and fervent from the first. The tears that flowed at Miletus, the heart that was nearly broken on his last journey to Jerusalem, the moving appeals and allusions of his epistles, and his capacity for ardent and constant friendships were not merely the growth of his mature years but were present, in seed at least, from his earliest childhood. He must always have been extremely sensitive to kindness, and the contrast between his remembrance of his friends after he became a Christian and his entire reticence about his parents and brothers or sisters shows how bitter and final was the disowning that followed his becoming a Christian. There is more than appears on the surface in his remark, "For whom I have suffered the loss of all things" (Phil. 3:8).

The zeal that led him to persecute the Church was already stirring in Paul's heart at a young age. "I am...a Jew," he once said, "born in Tarsus, a city in Cilicia...taught according to the perfect manner of the law of the fathers, and was zealous toward God" (Acts 22:3). Indeed, he tells us that he advanced in the Jewish religion beyond many of his own age among his countrymen, being more exceedingly zealous for the traditions of the fathers. Paul did not hold truth indolently or superficially or as a necessity of his early nurture and education but held truth as a solution that had saturated and dyed the deepest emotions of a very intense nature.

There was a sense in which he might have applied to himself some older words and said, "The zeal of thine house hath eaten me up" (John 2:17). May there not also have been an undefined hope that his zeal might atone for some of those defects of which he was so painfully conscious, commending him to God? He knew by personal experience what it was to have, as the rest of his brethren after the flesh, a zeal for God, but not according to knowledge.

As a child, Paul would learn by heart Deuteronomy 6:4–9 and Psalms 113—118. The years of his childhood would have passed like this: at the age of five he began to read the Scriptures; at six he would be sent to the school of a neighboring rabbi; at ten he would be instructed in the oral law; at thirteen he would become, by a kind of confirmation, a son of the law. But it is unlikely that he received the culture of the Greek philosophy, for which Tarsus was rather famous. This was rendered impossible by the uncompromising attitude of the Jews of the Dispersion to all the Gentile community around them. Between the ages of thirteen and sixteen, Paul would be sent to Jerusalem to pursue his training for the office of a rabbi, to which he was evidently designated by the ambition of his father. It was easy for Paul to do thus, since he had a married sister in

Jerusalem with whom he could stay during his attendance at the classes of the illustrious Gamaliel. "I am...brought up in this city," he said afterward, "at the feet of Gamaliel" (Acts 22:3).

We must not omit to record that during these boyish years he acquired a trade that would serve him usefully when hard pressed for means of livelihood. "He that teacheth not a trade is as though he taught his son to be a thief"—so ran the old Jewish proverb.

Every Jew was taught a trade, generally that of his father. Probably Paul's family for generations back had been engaged in weaving a dark coarse cloth of goat hair. From his childhood, Paul must have been familiar with the rattle of the looms, in which the long hair of the mountain goats was woven into a strong material suitable alike for the outer coats of craftsmen or for tents and known as Cilician cloth, after the name of the province in which Tarsus was situated. This handicraft was poorly remunerated, but in Paul's case, it was highly suitable to the demands of a wandering life. Other trades would require a settled workshop and expensive equipment, but this was a simple industry, capable of being pursued anywhere and needing the smallest possible equipment and tools.

From the confinement of a Roman prison, Paul had time to review his life of fifty years and those things that he had before counted gain. To the earnest gaze that he directed toward them, the receding shores of his early life came near again; and as he counted up their treasures, he wrote across them—*loss, dross:* "But what things were gain to me, those I counted loss for Christ. Yea doubtless, and I count all things but loss for the excellency of the knowledge of Christ Jesus my Lord" (Phil. 3:7–8).

It was not a small thing to have come of noble and godly parentage, to be a child of Abraham and heir of the promises made to his seed. *But Paul counted it loss.*

It was not a small thing to have built up by constant obedience and scrupulous care a fabric of blameless reputation. *But Paul counted it loss.*

It was not a small thing to be conscious of the throbbing of a fervent spirit that would tolerate no indolence or lethargy and that transformed duty to delight. *But Paul counted it dross.*

There was calm deliberation in his tone. Youth may be impassioned and hasty, but the man who speaks like this is not a youth. His life is covered with mature wisdom, and his heart is stored with the experience of several lives crowded into one. He has spent long years in prison, where there has been plenty of time for reflection and ample opportunity for weighing the past against the present. But notwithstanding all, and that the difficulties of the past are always minimized while those of the present are magnified, Paul twice over speaks of the advantages and achievements that had been the pride of his early manhood as loss and worse.

There was no irreverence in his allusions to the rites of the venerable system in which he had been nurtured. For long years, Judaism had been the only interpreter to him of the divine, the only nourishment of his spiritual instincts. The grounds of trust that he now deemed insufficient had at least been the landing places on the stairway of his upward ascent. He could not forget that God Himself had been the Architect of the house in which his soul had found a shelter and home, that His voice had spoken in the prophets, that His thoughts had inspired them, that His purposes had been fulfilled. No thoughtful man will talk contemptuously of his first book or of his first teachers. In these probably lay the rudiments of all he has afterward learned. But notwithstanding the noble reverence of the apostle's soul, Paul could not but affirm that what he had counted gain was loss.

The grounds for this verdict are probably to be found in two directions. On the one hand, Paul discovered that the sacrifices of Judaism, as was obvious from their constant repetition, might bring sins to remembrance, but they could not remove them; he discovered that outward rites, however punctiliously observed, did not avail to cleanse the conscience; he discovered that in Judaism there was no power unto salvation, nothing to reinforce and renew the flagging energies of the soul. On the other hand, he had found something better.

The young artist leaves his village home, inflated with pride at his achievements. Nothing like his work has ever been seen by the simple neighbors. They count him a prodigy, and he is only too glad to accept their estimate. In his secret judgment, he counts himself able to step forth into the arena of the world as a successful competitor for its prizes. So he goes forth, to Paris, to Milan, to Rome. But each month weakens his self-confidence and gives him a lower estimate of his abilities. Presently he becomes the pupil of some master artist, and when, after several years, he returns again to his home and opens the portfolio filled with the early studies, he closes it immediately with disgust. He wonders how he could ever have dared to count them art. What things were gain to him, those in the light of all that he has seen and learned, he now counts loss.

So Paul had seen Jesus. Before the glory of that heavenly vision, all other objects of attraction had paled. Paul counted all things to be loss for the excellency of the knowledge of Christ Jesus his Lord. In comparison with Jesus' finished work, all Paul's own efforts were futile. Paul felt relieved to turn from his own righteousness, based on the law, and to avail himself of God's method of righteousness, which was through faith in Christ. So long as he anticipated having to meet the demands of God's infinite holiness by his own endeavors, Paul was haunted with the dread that there might be some fatal flaw. But Paul learned that by renouncing all, he might gain Christ; that by forsaking his own efforts and trusting Christ, he might be found in Him, possessed of the flawless righteousness that had been wrought by His obedience unto death; that by confessing himself unable to do the good he would and identifying himself with the death of Christ, he might come to know the power of Christ's resurrection and attain day by day to something of its likeness. Then, with great thankfulness, Paul abandoned his own strivings and efforts and counted all his former gains but dross and dung, that he might win Christ and all that Christ could be and do.

It is an awful experience when the soul first awakes to find that it has been making a mistake in the most important of matters and has nearly missed the deepest meaning of life. It is frightening to discover that the rules it has made for itself and the structure of character it has laboriously built up are but wood, hay, and stubble. What a shock to learn that it has been building on an insecure foundation and that every brick must be taken down. Ah, me! It is a discovery that, when it comes in early manhood, for the moment at least, paralyzes—we fall to the ground and spend three days and nights stunned and dazed. When it comes at the end of life, we are of infinite regret. When it comes in the other world, it is black with the darkness of unutterable despair.

There is one test only that can really show whether we are right or wrong: it is our attitude toward Jesus Christ. If our spiritual life revolves around anything less than Him—though it be the doctrines of Christianity, work for Him, the rules of a holy life—it will inevitably disappoint and fail us. But if He is Alpha and Omega, if our faith, however feebly, looks up to Him, if we press on to know Him, the power of His resurrection, and the fellowship of His sufferings, if we count all things but loss for the excellency of His knowledge—we may walk in peace amid the mysteries of life and the lofty requirements of the great white throne.

3

Galatians 1:15

SEPARATED FROM BIRTH

What to thee is shadow, to Him is day
And the end He knoweth;
And not on a blind and aimless way,
The spirit goeth.

Like warp and woof, all destinies
Are woven fast,
Linked in sympathy, like the keys
Of an organ vast.

Whittier

When he became a man, Paul put away childish things (1 Cor. 13:11). But there were some things that he could not put away, and there was no need that he should, because they had been planned beforehand by God as a special qualification and preparation for his lifework. Over Paul's cradle in the crowded Jewish quarter of Tarsus, a divine purpose hovered. As to Jeremiah, so to him, the Word of the Lord might have come, saying, "Before I formed thee in the belly I knew thee; and before thou camest forth out of the womb I sanctified thee, and I ordained thee a prophet unto the nations" (Jer. 1:5). Paul had some inkling of this when he said, in writing to the Galatians, "But when it pleased God, who separated me from my mother's womb, and called me by his grace, to reveal his Son in me, that I might preach him among the heathen" (Gal. 1:15–16).

God has a purpose in every life, and when the soul is completely yielded and acquiescent, He will certainly realize it. Blessed is he who has never thwarted the working of the divine ideal.

One of the most interesting studies in a person's life is to see how all the circumstances and incidents of his initial stages have been shaped by a determining will and are made to subserve a beneficial purpose. Every thread is needed for the completed pattern, and every piece of equipment stands in good stead at the final test.

THE FUTURE APOSTLE MUST BE DEEPLY INSTRUCTED IN THE JEWISH LAW

The law must stand here as a convenient term not only for the moral and Levitical code as given in the Pentateuch but also for the minute and laborious additions of the rabbis, who—to use one of their own illustrations—had so overlaid the sweet flute of truth with their gilding as to silence its music. The righteousness of the law consisted in meats and drinks and diverse ordinances and washings, in the length of fringes and number of tassels, in the straining of wine lest there should be the dead body of a fly, in the tithing of the stalk as well as the flower of mint, in the punctilious measuring of the ground that not a step might be taken beyond the legitimate Sabbath day's journey. One great rabbi spent the whole week in considering how to observe the coming Sabbath.

No one could have appreciated the intolerable burden of this yoke of legalism—that even Peter said neither they nor their fathers were able to bear—unless he had been taught, as was Paul, "according to the perfect manner of the law of the fathers" (Acts 22:3). As Luther was reared in the Roman Catholic Church that he might appreciate the utter impotence of her system to pacify the conscience or appease the heart and that, having broken from it, he might show the way of escape to others, so Saul of Tarsus must experience the depths of which he speaks so often in the epistle to the Galatians, that he might be able to magnify the freedom wherewith Christ has made us free.

HE NEEDED TO BE AN EXPERT IN THE HEBREW SCRIPTURES

Every question in religious and ordinary Jewish life was settled by an appeal to the Scriptures. No speaker could gain the audience or hold the attention of a Jewish congregation for a moment unless he could show convincingly that his statements could be substantiated from the inspired Word. To the law and the testimony, every assertion must be brought. Before that venerable bar, every teacher must stand.

It was above all things necessary that Christianity should be shown to be not the destruction but the fulfillment of the ancient law—the white flower growing from the plant that God had brought from Ur of the Chaldees, the meridian day of which the dawn first streaked the sky at Moriah. What made Paul so "mad" against Christianity was its apparent denial and betrayal of the obvious meaning of Old Testament prophecies and types. Neither he nor any of his co-religionists were prepared to accept a humiliated, suffering, dying Messiah unless it could be shown without controversy that such a conception was the true reading of Moses, the prophets, and the law. Had any collection of sincere and earnest Jews been asked the question, "Ought not the Messiah to suffer such things and to enter into His glory?" they would have unhesitatingly answered no and would have required one who was thoroughly versed not only in Scripture but also in the obscure interpretations of the rabbi to prove to them from the entire range of the Old Testament that it required the Messiah to suffer.

This qualification also Paul acquired during his years of training under Gamaliel. Throughout the entire course, "the sacred oracles" were the only textbook, and every day was spent in the careful and minute consideration of words, lines, and letters, together with the interpretations of the various rabbis. Men might have chafed at Paul's renderings of the ancient words, but they could not dispute his intimate acquaintance with them and his profound scholarship. Paul knew the whole ground perfectly. There was not a single argument with which he was not familiar and for which he was not instantly ready with a reply. The field of Scripture had been repeatedly plowed over by that keen mind and its harvests gathered into that retentive memory. There are passages in Paul's writings that are little else than stairways of quotation, one built up from another. Paul's arguments are clenched by an appeal to the sacred Word, as though otherwise they would be inconclusive. For illustration he will go not to the illuminated book of nature, for which he seems to have had no eye, but to the incidents and narratives that have made the Old Testament the storybook of all the ages. It was this power that gave him an entrance into every synagogue and carried conviction to so many candid Jews. How richly, for instance, it was appreciated by Bible students, like those whom he met at Berea (Acts 17:11).

HE NEEDED TO HAVE
LARGE AND LIBERAL VIEWS

Jewish intolerance and exclusivism had built a high wall of partition between Jew and Gentile. The Jews had no dealings with the Samaritans; how much less with the Gentile dogs that crouched beneath the well-spread table of the children! Here is a characteristic saying of one of the doctors of the law: "If a Gentile fall into the sea, a Jew is not to pull him out; for it is written, Thou shalt not be guilty of thy neighbor's blood—but the Gentile is not thy neighbor."

The majority of the apostles were largely influenced by this caste spirit. It was hard for them, though they had been molded by the Lord Himself, to break through this exclusive fence of early training. Had the shaping of the primitive Church been left to them, though theoretically they might have acknowledged the equality of Jew and Gentile in God's sight, yet practically they would have drawn distinctions between the Jewish Christians and those other sheep whom their Shepherd was bringing but who were not of the Hebrew fold. Peter will go into a Gentile house and eat with the uncircumcised beneath the pressure of the heavenly vision, but when the glory of that memorable day has faded and certain men come down from James, he makes an excuse to withdraw into the impregnable fortress of Jewish superiority (Gal. 2:12). Evidently someone other than James or even Peter was needed who would dare to insist on the absolute equality of all who by faith had become stones in the one Church, buildings in the one holy temple, that was growing into a habitation for God. The need of a trumpet voice was urgent to proclaim that Jesus had abolished in His flesh the enmity, that He might "make in himself of twain one new man, so making peace" (Eph. 2:15). Through the ordering of divine providence, this qualification also was communicated to the future apostle of the uncircumcision.

By birth, as we have seen, Paul was a Hebrew. That was a prerequisite to have influence over Jews and to obtain admission into their synagogues. But Paul had been brought up at the feet of the great rabbi who, while reverenced as "the beauty of the law," was recognized also as the most large-hearted of all the Jewish doctors. As the grandson of the great teacher Hillel, Gamaliel was, as the story of the Acts indicates, one of the leaders of the Sanhedrin: "a doctor of the law, had in reputation among all the people" (Acts 5:34). But Gamaliel went so far as to permit and advocate the study of Greek literature. In his speech before the Sanhedrin (Acts 5), we trace the movements of a human and generous mind, willing to admit the workings of the divine Spirit beyond the limits of rigid orthodoxy and to follow the torch of truth wherever it might lead— a very holy man, deeply attached to the religion of his people yet accustomed to look at all questions from the standpoint of a large culture and wide charity.

The influence of such a teacher must have been very powerful on the young Tarsus student who had come to sit at his feet and regarded him with a boundless enthusiasm. Into the upturned furrows of that impressible nature may have been sown the seeds that under the sun of Christianity would ripen into such sayings as that "there is neither Jew nor Greek...for ye are all one in Christ Jesus" (Gal. 3:28).

HE NEEDED AN ESPECIALLY WIDE KNOWLEDGE OF THE WORLD

The man who is to be a missionary to men must know them. He who would be all things to all men, that by all means he might win some, must be familiar with their methods of life and thought. A Jerusalem Jew would have had a nearly impossible task of adapting himself to cultured Greeks and practical Romans, to barbarians and Scythians, to bond and free, to Festus the imperial governor and Agrippa the Hebrew king, to Onesimus the slave and Philemon the master, as did Paul.

But this qualification also was supplied without Paul's realizing its worth. From boyhood, Paul was familiar with the tides of Gentile life that flowed up the river Cydnus into his native city. Men from all over the world came here for purposes of trade. The wharves, baths, colonnades, and open places of the city were thronged with the costumes and rang with the many tongues of all the lands that touched on the great inland sea. And thus unconsciously the horizon of the boy's mind was widened to include the great outer world.

When his training at Jerusalem was complete, Paul must have returned to Tarsus. This surely must have been immediately before the appearance of John the Baptist preaching repentance in the Jordan valley. Paul could not have been in Judea at this time without making some reference to John's marvelous ministry and tragic end. In the same way, he must have missed the ministry and crucifixion of Jesus of Nazareth and the early years of the existence of the Church. But during this interval, his education was proceeding. In these years, he probably married, or he would not afterward have occupied a seat in the Sanhedrin. And he steadily pursued his trade or exercised his profession as a rabbi in the local synagogue or traveled far afield on some religious mission to make proselytes.

But imagine what those seven or eight years must have meant to the young Pharisee. Could the young athlete have restrained himself from encounters with the system of things surrounding him? There was a school of heathen philosophy in search of the supreme good: would he not try to debate its exponents? There was a vast system of idolatry, especially of Baal worship: would he not reason with its disciples, arguing that they cannot be gods that are made with hands? There was wild indulgence of shameless, sensual passion: would he not contrast it with the comparative purity of his own race? And all the while, he would be keenly observing and noting every phase of Gentile heathendom.

The pictures of the world of that age given in the first chapter to the Romans and the first epistle to the Corinthians and comprising such dark allusions to the depravity and abandonment of the Gentiles could have been given only by one who had obtained his information by personal observation. What vivid touches there are in his entreaty not to walk "as other Gentiles walk, in the vanity of their mind, having the understanding darkened, being alienated from the life of God...who being past feeling have given themselves over unto lasciviousness, to work all uncleanness with greediness" (Eph. 4:17–19).

HE MUST BE EQUIPPED WITH THE PREREQUISITES OF A GREAT TRAVELER

For this there were three necessary conditions: speech, safety, sustenance. And each was forthcoming.

Speech. Greek was the common language of the world, the medium of intercourse among educated persons, as English is today. And Paul was even more familiar with Greek than with the sacred Hebrew. When quoting the Scriptures, he habitually employed the Septuagint (i.e., the Greek) version. And he was able to speak their tongue fluently and elegantly enough to hold the attention of Athenian philosophers.

Safety. All the world was Roman. Roman governors in every province; Roman usages in every city; Roman coins, customs, and officials. To be a Roman citizen gave a man standing and position in any part of the empire. He might not be beaten without trial, or if he were, the magistrates were in jeopardy of losing their office and even their life. He could demand trial at the court of Caesar; if he appealed to Caesar, to Caesar he must go. He would be permitted to plead for himself before the court of Roman justice. So great were the advantages that men like Lysias, the chief captain, thought it worthwhile to purchase the right of freedom with a great sum (Acts 24:7). How great an advantage, then, to be able to say as Paul could, *I was free born!* Paul's family may have been originally settled in Tarsus as part of a Roman colony. Since Jews were always considered excellent colonists, this inestimable privilege came to cast its sheltering folds around its most illustrious son.

Sustenance. This also was secured to him. On whatever shore he was cast, there were always goats and always the demand for coarse cloth that he had been trained to produce from his boyhood.

In all this, how evidently was the divine purpose at work, shaping all things after the counsel of its own will. And what was true in Paul's case is as true for us all. A providence is shaping our ends; a plan is developing in our lives; a supremely wise and loving Being is making all things work together for good. In the sequel of our life's story, we shall see that there was a meaning and necessity in all the previous incidents, except those that were the result of our own folly and sin, and that even these have been made to contribute to the final result. Trust Him, child of God: He is leading you by a right way to the celestial city of habitation; and as from the terrace of eternity you review the path by which you came from the morning-land of childhood, you will confess that He has done all things well.

4

Acts 22:20

THY
MARTYR STEPHEN

He heeded not reviling tones,
Nor sold his heart to idle moans,
Tho' cursed, and scorn'd and bruised with stones.

But looking upward, full of grace,
He prayed, and from a happy place
God's glory smote him on the face.

Tennyson

*T*he method of God's introduction of His greatest servants to the world differs widely. In some cases, God's servants rise gradually and majestically, like the dawn, from the glimmer of childhood's early promise to the meridian of mature power and usefulness. In other cases, they flash like the lightning on the dark abyss of night. Sometimes God charges a man with a message and launches that man's career suddenly and irresistibly. Such a man was Elijah, with his "As the LORD of hosts liveth, before whom I stand" (1 Kings 18:15). Such a man was John the Baptist, with his "It is not lawful for thee to have thy brother's wife" (Mark 6:18). Such also was Savonarola of Florence; so also were many others called. And such was Stephen.

We know little or nothing of Stephen's beginnings. That he was a Hellenist Jew is almost certain, and that he had personally known and associated with the Son of Man, whom he afterward recognized in His glory, is more than probable. But of father, mother, birthplace, and education we know nothing. We have the story of one day, the record of one speech—that day his last, that speech his apology and defense for his life.

Stephen reminds us of a cloud, not especially distinguishable from its companions, that has helped to form the gray covering of the sky during an overcast afternoon. We would not have noticed it—indeed, the sun would have set without even touching it—but when the orb of day has passed beneath the horizon, the cloud catches its departing rays and becomes saturated and steeped with fire. See how it burns with glory! Its very heart is turned to flame! For a few moments the light remains, and it is gone! So Stephen caught for a brief space the glory of the departed Lord and, reflecting it, was transformed into the same image: "And all that sat in the council, looking stedfastly on him, saw his face as it had been the face of an angel" (Acts 6:15).

Stephen's life and death must always have attracted reverent interest, but how much more so as we trace his influence on the method, thought, and character of the great apostle, whose lifework it became to perpetuate and render permanent what was rarest and noblest in the Church's first deacon and martyr.

THE MOVEMENT OF WHICH STEPHEN WAS THE PRODUCT

Three streams of thoughts were meeting in tumultuous eddies in Jerusalem.

There were *the Jews of the Pharisee party,* represented by Gamaliel, Saul of Tarsus, and other notable men. They were characterized by an intense religiousness that encompassed their ancestry, their initial rite, their law, their temple. Were they not Abraham's children? Had not God entered into special covenant relations with them, of which circumcision was the outward sign and seal? Were they not zealous in their observance of the law that had been uttered amid the thunder peals of Sinai, not for themselves alone but for the world? Had not their rabbis added to the law an immense number of minute and careful regulations to which they yielded scrupulous and anxious obedience? And as for the temple, the whole of their national life was anchored to the spot where it stood. There was the only altar, priesthood, shrine, of which their religion admitted. Though the temple might be a den of thieves and Jerusalem full of uncleanness, they felt that no harm could befall them, no fiery storm overwhelm. Like their forefathers in Jeremiah's days, they trusted in lying words, saying, "The temple of the Lord, The temple of the Lord, The temple of the Lord, are these" (Jer. 7:4). But they had no thought of amending their ways and their doings. Narrow, theological, bigoted, intensely fanatical, priding themselves on their national privilege as the chosen people but resentful against the appeals of the greatest of their prophets, counting on the efficacy of their system but careless of personal character—such was the orthodox and conservative Jewish party of the time.

Next came the *Hebrew Christian Church,* led and represented by the apostles. To culture and eloquence they laid no claim. Of founding a new religious organization, they had no idea. That they should ever live to see Judaism superseded by the teaching they were giving or Christianity existing apart from the system in which they had been nurtured was a thought that, in the furthest flights of their imagination, never occurred to them. Their Master had rigorously observed the Jewish rights and feasts, and they followed in His steps and conveyed a similar course of action on their adherents. The Church lingered still in the portals of the synagogue. The disciples observed the hours of prayer, were found in devout attendance at the temple's services, had their children circumcised, and would not have dreamed of being released from the regulations that bound the ordinary Jews as with iron chains. And it seems certain that if nothing had happened of the nature of Stephen's apology and protests, the Church would have become another Jewish sect, distinguished by the piety and purity of its adherents and by their strange belief in the Messiahship of Jesus of Nazareth, who had been crucified under Pontius Pilate.

Lastly, there were *the converts from among the Hellenist Jews.* In Acts 6:1, they are distinctly referred to. In verse 9, the various synagogues in which they customarily met are enumerated—of these Stephen was the holy and eloquent spokesperson.

The origin of the Hellenist, or Grecian, Jews must be traced back to the captivity that God overruled to promote the dissemination of

Jewish ideals throughout the world. It was but a small contingent that returned to Jerusalem with Nehemiah and Ezra. The vast majority of dispersed Jews elected to remain in the land of their adoption for purposes of trade. They slowly spread throughout Asia Minor to the cities of its seaboard and the highland districts of its interior, planting everywhere the synagogue, with its declaration on behalf of the unity and the spirituality of God. Egypt, and especially Alexandria; Greece, with her busy commercial seaports; Rome, with her imperial cosmopolitan influence—all became familiar with the peculiar physical features and customs of this wonderful people who always contrived to secure for themselves a large share of the wealth of any country in which they had settled. But their free contact with the populace of many lands resulted in a remarkable change in them.

While the Jews of Jerusalem and Judea shrank from the defiling touch of heathenism and built higher the wall of separation, growing continually prouder, more bitter, more narrow, the Jews who were scattered through the world became more liberal and cosmopolitan. They dropped their Hebrew mother tongue for Greek. They read the Septuagint version of the Scriptures. Their children were influenced by Greek culture and philosophy. They became able to appreciate the purposes of God moving through the channels of universal history. They learned that though their fathers had received the holy oracles for mankind, God had nowhere left Himself without witness. Compelled, as they were, to relinquish the temple with its holy rites except on rare and great occasions when they traveled from the ends of the earth to be present at some great festival, they magnified in its place the synagogue, with its worship, its reading of the law, its words of exhortation. And they welcomed to its precincts all who cared to avail themselves of its privileges and to set their faces toward the God of Abraham. Many of these open-minded Hellenist Jews, when they retired from their years in successful trade, came back and settled in Jerusalem. The different countries from which they hailed were represented by special synagogues: one of the Libertines who had been freed from slavery, one of the Cyrenians, one of the Alexandrians, one of them of Cilicia and of Asia. The mention of the latter is specially interesting when we recall that the chief city of Cilicia was Tarsus.

After some years of absence, Saul returned to settle at

Jerusalem. It is possible that the city's Jewish leaders, having been impressed by Saul's remarkable talents and enthusiastic devotion to Judaism, had summoned Saul to take part in or lead the opposition to Christianity, to which events were daily more irrevocably committing them. It is almost certain, also, that to facilitate his operations, Saul was at this time nominated to a seat in the Sanhedrin, enabling him to give his vote against the followers of Jesus (Acts 26:10).

Saul's first impressions about the followers of "the Way," as the early disciples were termed, were wholly unfavorable. It seemed to Saul sheer madness to suppose that the crucified Nazarene could be the long-looked-for Messiah or that He had risen from the dead. Saul, therefore, threw himself into the breach and took the lead in disputing with Stephen, who had just been raised to office in the young church. Not content with the conservative and timid attitude that the apostles had preserved for some five years, Stephen was now leading an aggressive and forward policy.

THE BURDEN OF STEPHEN'S TESTIMONY

The power of the testimony that Stephen gave with such wisdom and grace in the synagogues of Jerusalem, and especially in the Cilician, may be gathered from his apology that, while touching chords that vibrated most deeply in the hearts of his hearers, was intended as his own vindication and defense. It is a marvelous address, the whole meaning of which can be realized only when Stephen's position and circumstances are borne in mind. It was the first attempt to read the story of God's dealings with Israel in the light of Christ, the earliest commentary on the Old Testament by the New, the fragmentary draft of the epistle to the Hebrews, the suggestion to at least one of his hearers of a deeper way of studying the lessons of the law. The mystery that had been hidden from ages and generations—and that was probably still hidden even from the apostles—was made known to this Christian Hellenist Jew. Stephen's eyes were the first that were opened to see that the old covenant was becoming old and was near to vanishing away because it was on the point of being superseded by that better hope through which all men might draw near to God.

Can we not imagine those eager disputings in the Cilician synagogue between these two ardent and vehement spirits, close akin at heart, as the future would show, though now apparently so far divided. Each thoroughly versed in Scripture, each agile in argument and strong of soul, each devoted to the holy traditions of the past; but the one was blinded by an impenetrable veil, while to the other, heaven was open and the Son of Man was revealed standing at the right hand of God.

Like most who speak God's truth for the first time, Stephen was greatly misunderstood. We gather this from the charges made against him by the false witnesses, whom the Sanhedrin incited by way of bribery. These false witnesses accused Stephen of uttering blasphemous words against Moses, of speaking against the temple and the law, of declaring that Jesus of Nazareth would destroy the temple and change customs delivered by Moses. And as we attentively follow Stephen's argument, we can see how it was that these impressions had been caused.

Saul would lecture on the glories of the temple, standing on the site where for centuries Jehovah had been worshiped. But Stephen would insist that any holy soul might worship God in the temple of his own soul, that there was no temple in the old time when God spoke to Abraham and the patriarchs, that David was discouraged from building one, and that at the time of the temple's dedication, Solomon expressly acknowledged that God did not dwell in temples made with hands.

Saul would insist on the necessity of the rite of circumcision. But Stephen would argue that it could not be all-important, since God made promises to Abraham long before that rite was instituted.

Saul would show the unlikelihood of Jesus being God's Deliverer because Jesus was unrecognized by the leaders and shepherds of Israel. Stephen would rejoin that there was nothing extraordinary in this, since Joseph had been sold for jealousy and Moses rejected on three distinct occasions: "Which of the prophets have not your fathers persecuted?" (Acts 7:52).

Saul said that all the prophets pointed to the glorious advent of the Messiah. Stephen reviewed Moses, the prophets, and the psalms and showed that they required that Christ should suffer.

Saul affirmed that nothing could supersede Moses. Stephen quoted Moses himself as asserting that the Lord God would raise up a greater prophet than himself.

All this Stephen affirmed with the greatest reverence and awe. He spoke of the God of Glory, of the great ones of the past as "our fathers," of the angel that spoke at Sinai, and of the living oracles of Scripture. And yet it is undeniable that he saw with undimmed vision that Jesus of Nazareth must change the customs that Moses delivered and lead His Church into more spiritual aspects of truth.

How little Stephen could have known that he was dropping seeds into the heart of his chief opponent that were to bear harvests to one hundredfold—nay, to many millionfold—through the centuries and in the broad harvest field of the world! Thus, a plant may yield one white flower, but the seeds it drops may live and bloom again in uncounted springs.

But as the battle rose and fell within the walls of that Cilician synagogue, it was an amazing conflict. Here ancient authority, there individual responsibility. Here the bondage of the letter, there the freedom of the spirit. Here the priest and ecclesiastic, there the Spirit-taught and led of God. Here bigotry and pride, there humility and insight. Here the shackles of the prison of the soul, there the open heaven. In miniature it was the battle of all the ages, the one eternal conflict between form and spirit, between a false religiousness and the religion of the soul that stands unveiled before God.

HIS MARTYRDOM

We know little of Stephen's life. It was more than probable, as we have already said, that Stephen knew Jesus in His earthly life, for he instantly recognized Him in the heavenly vision. Perhaps Stephen had followed Him during the latter part of His ministry. Stephen could at least describe Him as the Righteous or Just One, as though he had had ample opportunity of appraising His blameless worth. Surely he must have seen Him die, for the traits of His dying beauty molded Stephen's own last hours. How meekly to bear his cross, to plead for his murderers with a divine charity, to breathe his departing spirit into unseen hands, to find in death the gate of life and, amid the horror of a public execution, the secret of calm and peace—all these were rays of light caught from the cross where his Master had poured out His soul unto death.

This, too, powerfully affected Saul (Paul). That light on the martyr's face, that evident glimpse into the unseen Holy, those words, that patience and forgiveness, that peace encompassing his mangled body, crushed and bleeding, as he fell asleep—Paul could never forget them. Long years after, when a similar scene of hate was surrounding him, Paul reverted to Christ's martyr, Stephen, and counted it a high honor meekly to follow in his steps. Not only did Paul shape his own great speeches on the model of that never-to-be-forgotten address, not only did those conceptions of the spiritual nature of Christ's kingdom affect Paul's whole upcoming teaching and ministry, but the very light that radiated from that strong, sweet, noble character of Stephen seemed to have been absorbed by Paul's spirit, to be radiated forth again in much patience, in afflictions, in necessities, in distresses, in strifes, in tumults, in pureness, in knowledge, in longsuffering, in kindness, in the Holy Spirit, in love unfeigned.

It is thus that the martyr Church has ever overcome by the word of her testimony because the saints have loved not their lives even unto death. The blood of the martyrs is the seed of the Church. The destruction of the flower is the scattering of its pollen. The hammer is broken on its anvil. The power of the persecutor is overcome by the patience of his victims. Saul, at whose feet witnesses lay down their clothes, is catching up and assuming the mantle of the departing prophet and saint.

5

Acts 26:13

A Light
From Heaven

As to Thy last Apostle's heart
Thy lightning glance did then impart
Zeal's never-dying fire.

Keble

If the importance of events can be estimated by the amount of space given in Scripture to their narration, the transformation upon the career of Saul of Tarsus from the visitation of the risen Lord must take second place in the story of the New Testament. It is described three times, with great minuteness of detail—first by Luke and twice by Paul—and the narration occupies more space than the story of any other event except the crucifixion of our Lord.

This must be accounted for partly because of the important part played by the apostle in the shaping of the early Church and partly because Saul's conversion was due to the personal agency of the risen Lord, who appeared as literally as during any of His appearances after the resurrection. This was not a vision like John had

43

when he was in the Spirit (Rev. 1:10), nor was it a mere transient impression on the sensitive plate of the imagination, no fading, dreamlike fancy. It was a manifestation of the risen Lord, like that which won the faith of Thomas.

It was one of the deepest convictions of the apostle throughout the rest of his life that he had veritably and certainly seen the Lord, and he was therefore as empowered to be a witness of Jesus' resurrection as any who had accompanied the Lord, beginning from the baptism of John until the day that Jesus was received up. "Am I not an apostle? am I not free? have I not seen Jesus Christ our Lord?" Paul asks (1 Cor. 9:1). And after enumerating the Lord's appearances after His resurrection, Paul adds, placing that scene on the road to Damascus on a level with the rest, "And last of all he was seen of me also, as of one born out of due time" (1 Cor. 15:8). Ananias used the same phrase when, entering the darkened chamber where the apostle lay like an eagle with a broken wing, he said "The Lord, even Jesus, that appeared unto thee in the way as thou camest, hath sent me" (Acts 9:17).

Six days before, Saul had left Jerusalem with a small retinue furnished as his escort by the high priest. The journey was long and lonely, giving time for reflection, of which he had known but little during the crowding events of the previous months. He had been too closely occupied by those ruthless house visits, those constant trials, those scourgings, tortures, and martyrdoms; and in the incessant occupation, he had been drifting with the rush of events without taking his bearings or realizing their precise direction.

It was high noon. Unlike most travelers, Saul refused to spend even an hour in the retirement of his tent for shelter from the downward rays of the sun, piercing like swords, while all the air was breathless with the heat. He was too weary of his own musings, too eager to be at his work. Suddenly the little cavalcade left the stony wastes over which the track had lain and began to pass beneath "the flickering shadows of ancient olives," while Damascus suddenly came into view amid a soft haze of green vegetation. Its gardens, orchards, and groves made an emerald setting for its terraced roofs and white glistening cupolas.

The goal of the long journey was well in sight. Within an hour or two, he would be within the gates and traversing the street called Straight to deliver his commission to the authorities and to ascertain the best point for commencing proceedings. But suddenly a great light—above the brightness of the Syrian noontide sun—shone around him; and a voice, amid the blaze, unintelligible and inarticulate to his companions though clear enough to him, was heard speaking in the familiar Aramaic and calling him by name (Acts 26:14).

There can be no doubt, in the light of the passages we have noticed, as to the origin of that light—it came straight from the face of the glorified Savior. With a similar light, it had become illumined on the Mount of Transfiguration, when His face did shine as the sun, His garments grew white as the light (Matt. 17:2), and all the snows around reflected the golden sheen. Something of the same beauty and splendor was described by John in later years when he tells of the revelation given him in Patmos, but even this must have fallen far behind the Master's actual appearance on the way to Damascus. In the one case, His countenance was as when the sun shines in his strength; in the other, its glory was above the brightness of the sun.

In the light of that moment, the apostle saw many things. It was like a sudden flashlight flung over an abyss, revealing secret things that had been entirely hidden or but dimly understood.

In the glory of that light Paul became convinced of the truth of Christianity. His objection to Christianity was not that Jesus of Nazareth had been crucified. Had this been all, the young Pharisee would have respected Him. His blameless life, His teaching of the spirituality and unity of the divine nature, His belief in the resurrection of the dead, His fearless exposure of what was false and vicious, would even have attracted Paul's admiration. But it was intolerable that He should pose as the Messiah or that His followers should charge the rulers with the murder of the long-expected King.

Only one thing could convince Paul. He must have evidence: he must see this Jesus of Nazareth, whom he knew to have been crucified, living on the other side of death; he must be able to recognize and establish His identity; he must hear Him speak. Such evidence given to him would be conclusive, but nothing less would avail. If from heaven the Man of Nazareth and the cross were to speak to Paul—radiant with light, exerting divine power—Paul's objections would be scattered, and with another of his followers he would be compelled to cry, "My Lord and my God" (John 20:28).

This very revelation was made to Paul. It could not be a dream, a vision, or a hallucination. Paul was too sane to base the entire change of his career upon anything so flimsy. And in his writings, Paul always distinguishes between such mental images and that appearance of the Lord on the road to Damascus. As Barnabas said afterward, by way of explanation to the apostles, "he had seen the Lord in the way, and that he had spoken to him" (Acts 9:27). Paul felt instantly that his life must have a new meaning and purpose, and he must live to establish the faith of which he had made such determined havoc.

In the glory of that light Paul beheld the supreme revelation of God. Nature had told something of God. His glory had shone from rolling worlds and from the outspread expanse of oceans and seas, had covered morning skies with daffodil and evening clouds with crimson and gold, had goldened in the harvest fields and kindled around bush and flower and thicket. From the beginning, God had not left Himself without a witness, in that He did good and gave rains from heaven and fruitful seasons, filling men's hearts with food and gladness. "The heavens declare the glory of God; and the firmament sheweth his handywork. Day unto day uttereth speech, and night unto night sheweth knowledge. There is no speech nor language, where their voice is not heard" (Ps. 19:1-3). Thus, through the things that had been made, the invisible things of God had been revealed, even His everlasting power and divinity. But *this* light near Damascus was above the brightness of the sun and made all nature's wonders pale as stars at dawn.

There had been a further revelation to Israel. The light that shone on the face of Moses was emblematic of the fuller disclosures of Himself that God gave to His chosen people. So excellent was that light that the children of Israel could not look upon Moses for the glory of his face, and he was finally compelled to cover it with a veil. But that veil also had become emblematic of the blindness of Israel to the greatness of the revelation made to them.

But the glory of God on the face of Jesus was above the brightness of any previous dispensation. That was of the letter, this of the spirit; that was the ministration of death, this of life; that was temporary and passed away, this was the final and permanent outshining of the love of God. There is no conceivable method of divine manifestation that can excel the light that shines from the face of Jesus. They were human features that looked down on the Jewish persecutor through the open doorway of heaven, but they were aglow with the light of the Shekinah that passed between the pieces of Abraham's sacrifices, shone in the burning bush, lighted the march of Israel through the Red Sea, and at the dedication of Solomon's temple drove the priests before its waves of billowy glory from the holy place into the outer court. Paul beheld the glory of God in the face of Jesus whom he had persecuted.

Would you know God? You must study Him in Jesus. So utterly did the Son of Man renounce His own words and works and will that we know comparatively little of Him. All was from the Father and to the Father. The words He spoke were the Father's; the works He wrought, the Father's; the reconciliation perfected for erring man, achieved through Him by the Father, who was "in Christ, reconciling the world unto himself" (2 Cor. 5:19). We need nothing behind this; there is nothing behind. In heaven itself we shall still behold the light of the glory of God in the face of Jesus, our eyes getting stronger to bear it, our insight being always deeper and more perfect. That light shone before the first ray of sunlight gleamed over the abyss, and it will shine when sun, moon, and stars are dark and cold.

That Light Revealed Paul's Real Warfare

The earliest name of the new sect, as we have seen, was *the Way*. In later years, the apostle was proud to adopt and use it: "I confess unto thee, that after the way which they call heresy, so worship I the God of my fathers" (Acts 24:14). It was an arousing and significant title. These simple souls had found a new and living way to the knowledge and worship of God, consecrated through the torn flesh of Him whom their chief priests and rulers had delivered up to be condemned to death.

The young man Saul was exceedingly angry against the pilgrims of the Way. He made havoc of them, and the Greek word is descriptive of wild boars uprooting tender vines. He devastated them with the fury of an invading army. Not content with attacks on their public meetings, Saul paid visits to their homes, dragging out the patient, holy women as well as the uncomplaining men, scourging them, thrusting them in prison, putting them to death, and compelling them to blaspheme the holy name by which they were called. He breathed out threatening and slaughter, as a cruel monster might snort fire. He was so enraged against them that when the church at Jerusalem lay desolate and its garden was torn and trampled into a desert, he pursued the same methods in distant cities; and on the present memorable occasion, he had received letters to bring to Jerusalem those of the Way who were there in bonds to be punished.

Great prospects began then to unfold before the persecutor, and though his tender nature must have revolted from his sanguinary and ruthless efforts, though the sight of suffering inflicted at his instigation must have been very abhorrent, he was incited to pursue the path he had entered by the enthusiastic praises of his co-religionists.

There was, however, a deeper motive at work. "I verily thought...that I ought" (Acts 26:9). This work of extermination seemed to him part of his religious duty. He owed it to God to stamp out the followers of Jesus, and the more revolting it was to his nature, the more meritorious it was in the sight of heaven. Might not these efforts atone for any coming short in respect to the demands of God's law, which now and again forced itself home on his inner consciousness? Might not his victory over the reluctance of his heart be expiratory and atone for many failures? But, like the Roman soldiers who crucified the Lord, he knew not what he did: "[I] was before a blasphemer, and a persecutor, and injurious: but I obtained mercy, because I did it ignorantly in unbelief" (1 Tim. 1:13).

As, however, that light fell upon his path, Paul suddenly awoke to discover that instead of serving God he was colliding with Him and was actually uprooting and ravaging that for which the Son of His love had expended tears and blood. In persecuting the sect of the Nazarenes, Paul was persecuting the Son of God. By every blow he struck at the infant Church, he was lacerating those hands and piercing that side. By every sigh and groan extorted from the members of Christ's Body, he had elicited from the Head in heaven the remonstrance, "Saul, Saul, why persecutest thou me?" (Acts 9:4). It was a terrible and overwhelming discovery. The earth seemed to yawn before him. Somehow his religion had brought him into collision with God in the person of those who were dear to Him, and evidently, instead of their being wrong and he right, they were right and he was wrong. Instead of his fanatical zeal being pleasing to God, it was grievous to Him and heaping up wrath against a day of wrath. Ah, it is an awful discovery when a great light from heaven shows a man that what he has regarded his solemn duty has been one long sin against the dearest purposes of God!

THAT LIGHT ALSO REVEALED THE INADEQUACY OF PAUL'S RELIGIOUS LIFE

Paul had lived out all that he thought to be right. There was no prescription of the elders to which he had not conformed. So far as he knew what religion prescribed, he was blameless. Indeed, had he not gone beyond its prescriptions in the zeal with which he had harried the Church? But of late he had been compelled to confess to a dull sense of uneasiness and dissatisfaction. He studiously fought against it by immersing himself more diligently than ever in the work of persecution, yet there it was, and sometimes the evil thing (as he thought it) cast a petrifying glance upon his utmost efforts.

Two causes further instigated his uneasiness. First, he felt that his religion did not satisfy him. It gave him no such tender views of the love of God as had impressed Moses or Daniel, and it seemed ineffective to curb the imperious demands of sin. Often the good he would he did not, while the evil he hated he did (Rom. 7:19). Often he felt himself a captive, sold under sin. Often he cried aloud that he was a wretched man bound to an intolerable yoke that chafed him to the depths. And there seemed no deliverance. Always those cases of minute questions of conscience, always the same exactions of outward obedience, always the same weary sense of failure as the attempt to spend one day of perfect obedience was reviewed from the evening hour. Was there nothing better?

Second, it seemed as though these humble disciples of Jesus of Nazareth had something better. The meekness with which they bore their sufferings was far removed from obstinacy. The purity of their home life vindicated their professions. The light that shone upon their dying faces and the prayers for their persecutors, which they offered with their dying breath, evidenced the possession of a secret of which he knew that he was destitute. Could that religion be right that threw him into antagonism with such lovely traits and characteristics? Besides, he had often heard them speaking of their Teacher, His life of beneficence, His pure and lofty teachings, His maxims for the regulation of the inner life, His directions for the behavior of His followers—and when they did so, they touched chords that responded deep down in his soul. It seemed to him sometimes as though this Nazarene had discovered the pearl of great price and held the secret of a blessed life. Yet how could He be the Messiah who had come to such an end! And how absurd it was to say that He had risen, when the Roman sentries had solemnly testified that His body had been stolen by His disciples while they slept.

But all these questionings about his religious life were brought to a head and confirmed when suddenly he beheld Jesus of Nazareth enthroned on the right hand of power and shining with a light above the brightness of the sun. What could he say of a righteousness that had led him to reject and persecute the Son of God? Of what value was it? Surely that which had led him to reject and persecute the Son of God Himself in the persons of His servants must have been a deadly and pernicious delusion. He had thought himself blameless, but in the beam of that light, he discovered that he was of all sinners the chief, that he was not worthy to be called a son, and that he might be thankful if he were numbered among the hired servants.

HE ALSO DISCOVERED THE SOURCE OF HIS UNEASINESS OF HEART AND CONSCIENCE

Before, he may have attributed it to a morbid and melancholic element in his constitution, to the reaction of his mind from the sight of suffering, to a weakness of which he should rid himself as quickly as possible. He now saw that these were the prickings of the great Shepherd's stick, by which He had long been attempting to bring him into that attitude and lead him to undertake the lifework that had been prepared for him from the foundation of the world.

When the Master said, "It is hard for thee to kick against the pricks" (Acts 9:5), His speech gave Him away. It was said of Him during His earthly ministry that without a parable He did not speak to His people. Now from heaven His lips took up the wonted strain. He likened Himself to one who had purchased a young heifer at a great price. He has brought it into the field to pull the plow in a certain direction, but it resists and seeks another, compelling its owner to use the sharply pointed goad, pressing it against its flanks till it obeys his will. Saul suddenly awoke to find that he had been purchased by the Lord, who had been seeking for a long time to make him take the predestined track, and that all the bitter remorse of conscience had been intended for this sole purpose. It was a new conception of the religious life. Henceforth, he was not to do his own prompting, but to do God's; not to be clothed in his own righteousness, but to be clothed in God's; not to cut up and destroy, but to construct; not to oppose the Nazarene, but to take His yoke, to bear His burden, to do His will.

THAT LIGHT ALSO REVEALED TO HIM THE COURSE OF HIS FUTURE

Henceforth, Paul was to be a minister and a witness of those things that he had seen and of those in which Christ would still appear to him. All that was required of him was to live in unbroken accord with the risen Savior, beholding His beauty, inquiring in His temple, receiving His messages for transmission to others. It was enough. He meekly asked what he must do, what the new and rightful Master of his life would have him *do*. And in answer, he was told to take the next step that lay just before him, allowing himself to be led into the city. He little understood how great things he would have to *suffer* (Acts 9:16). These were a secret that Christ whispered in the ear of His friend, Ananias. It would be enough for the new convert to learn it afterward. After all, men accomplish as much by suffering as by active toil, and the world owes as much to the anguish of its martyrs as to the words and deeds of its apologists and workers.

And then there arose before him, in a flash on the high road and in the fuller development during the three days' retirement in the house of Judas, the Lord's desire for his life—that he should be sent to Jew and Gentile, that by his simple witness he would be used to open blind eyes, that men might turn from darkness to light, from the power of Satan unto God, so as to receive remission of sin and inheritance among the sanctified. That conception molded Paul's life, lingered always in Paul's memory, and formed the basis of one of Paul's noblest outbursts (Col. 1).

To know the divine will, to see the Righteous One, to hear His voice, to be His witness and chosen vessel, to bear His name before Gentiles and kings and the children of Israel—such was henceforth the prize of the mark of his high calling toward which Paul began to press (Acts 9:15, 22:14–15). Paul felt that he had been apprehended; he realized something of the purpose for which he had been apprehended; and with patient faith he resolved, so far as in him lay, to apprehend it.

How could he be other than obedient to the heavenly vision that summoned him to a life of self-sacrificing toil? As a token of his meek submission he allowed his fellow travelers to lead him by the hand into the city where he had expected to enter as an inquisitor, and he bent low to receive instruction from one of those simple-hearted believers whom he had expected to drag captive to Jerusalem. Such are the triumphs of the grace of God, and in Paul's case, it was shown to be exceedingly abundant.

6

Galatians 1:15–17

THE INNER REVELATION OF CHRIST

The proudest heart that ever beat,
Hath been subdued in me;
The wildest will that ever rose—
To scorn thy cause, or aid thy foes—
Is quelled, my God, by Thee!

Thy will, and not my will, be done;
Henceforth I'd be for ever thine;
Confessing Thee, the living Word,
My Savior Christ, my God, my Lord,
Thy Cross shall be my sign!

W. Hone

*I*n these wonderful verses of Galatians we have an epitome of the apostle Paul's life. There is, first, his separation in the divine purpose before his birth for the high and blessed work of ministering the gospel. Then there is his vocation by the grace of God, when a voice called to him that his prepared ear detected, though to others it was as thunder. These are followed by three successive steps: the revelation of Christ, the ministration of human sympathy and help, and Paul's isolation in Arabia. And finally, to crown all, there is afforded an indication of his lifework of preaching among the Gentiles the unsearchable riches of Christ.

How different to his anticipation was Saul's entrance into Damascus! He had probably often solaced himself during his weary six days' journey by picturing the reception that would be accorded to him by the authorities at Damascus on his arrival at their city as the Commissioner of the High Priest, charged with the destruction of the Nazarene heresy. But instead of honor, there was consternation and surprise. No one could quite explain or understand what had taken place. Dismounted from his horse, Saul went afoot. Instead of the haughty bearing of the inquisitor, the helplessness of a sightless man appealed for hands to lead him. Shrinking from notice and welcome, he was only too eager to reach a lonely chamber, where he might recover from the awful effects of that collision between his mortal and sinful nature and the holy, glorious Son of God, whom he had so ruthlessly persecuted.

"Trembling and astonished" (Acts 9:6), Saul seemed a stricken, dejected, broken man—but his soul was radiant with the light of the glory of God in the face of Jesus. The fire that shone in the burning bush had suddenly kindled upon him. As a lightning flash illumines the ink-black night, revealing the precipice toward which the traveler was stumbling and unveiling for one brief instant the city with its glistening buildings or the country with its expanse of forest, river, and pastureland, so in a moment he had seen God, Christ, the Old Testament Scriptures, and the mistaken purpose of his life.

It is interesting to notice how many seeds of the teaching that the apostle gave out in later days may be discovered in the records of his conversion.

"I am Jesus whom thou persecutest" (Acts 26:15): *there* is the believer's identification with the Lord, involving all that wonderful teaching of the oneness of the Head and members.

"To make thee a minister and a witness" (Acts 26:16): *there* is the origin of his constant reference to witness and testimony bearing.

"The Gentiles, unto whom now I send thee" (Acts 16:17): *on this* he rested his claim to be considered specially the apostle of the Gentiles, and perhaps at this time, those two great revelations may have passed for a moment before the eyes of his heart, to be elaborated in later years. The one revelation was that the Gentiles should be fellow members, fellow heirs, and fellow partakers with the chosen nation in all the privileges and rights of the gospel. The other revelation was to make all men see what is the fellowship of the mystery that from eternal ages has been hidden in the heart of God—the riches of the glory of this mystery, which is Christ in you, the hope of glory—that even the hearts of Gentiles may become the dwelling place and temple of the living Savior (Eph. 3; Col. 1).

In Acts 26:17–18, we find an epitome of the first chapter of the epistle to the Colossians. It is, in fact, the embryo of the apostle's thoughts on the justification and sanctification of the soul. The whole of his message might be focused around these two points: remission of sins and an inheritance among the sanctified through faith in the living Christ.

At this formative period in his life, three effective agencies were brought to bear on him: the work of God on his heart, contact with Ananias, and the education of the desert solitudes.

THE WORK OF GOD ON HIS HEART

"It pleased God...to reveal his Son in me" (Gal. 1:15–16). The apostle knew too much of the divine life to admit that the vast change in him could be entirely accounted for by what he had seen with his mortal and now blinded eyes. He was aware that a true and lasting work can be achieved only when the inner eye has perceived things that are hidden from mortal sense. In other words, God, who commanded the light to shine out of darkness, must shine *in the heart* to give the light of the knowledge of His glory in the face of Jesus (2 Cor. 4:6).

Imagine the abundance of revelations made to the blinded man during those three days and nights of silence and solitude in the house of Judas. Is it wonderful that he became totally unaware of the needs of the body and did not eat or drink? There are hours when we lose all consciousness of earth and already live in the heavenlies, when the soul loses count of the moments, sets sail from the coastline of earth, and finds itself out on the broad bosom of the ocean of eternity. Such was the experience of this soul.

What mysteries began to pass before him like the procession of the divine nature as God proclaimed His name to Moses down the mountain gorge! We talk about discovery; we should rather speak of disclosure. Is there such a thing as discovery? Is it not rather true of all invention, of all fresh readings of nature, that God is taking man up into the mountain of vision and showing him the things that have been and are and shall be, bidding him write them in a book for the generations to come? During those wondrous hours, God unveiled secrets that had been kept in silence through times eternal but were manifested to Saul according to the commandment of the eternal God, that he might make them known unto all nations, unto obedience of faith.

But the crowning revelation of all was that on which Paul places special emphasis. It was amazing to learn that Jesus of Nazareth was in very deed the Son of the Highest and that the Christ must suffer and be the first by His resurrection from the dead to proclaim light unto the people and the Gentiles. It was amazing to be taught that remission of sins and the heritage of a holy life were the gift of God to the open hand of faith. It was amazing to discover that there was no distinction between Jew and Greek, but that the same God was Lord of all and rich to all. But what was most amazing of all was the unveiling of the indwelling Christ, living literally within Paul by His Spirit, so that while he was in Christ, Christ was also in him, as the branch has its place in the vine and the vine lives through the branch.

O soul of man, has this revelation ever been your experience? Do you know that Christ is in you? If you truly believe in Him, there is no doubt of it. "Know ye not your own selves, how that Jesus Christ is in you, except ye be reprobates" (2 Cor. 13:5). And yet you may be in ignorance of this transcendent possession. Ask God to reveal His Son in you, to make you know experientially the riches of the glory of this mystery. He will rend the veil of the inner life in two from the top to the bottom and in the most holy place of your spirit disclose the Shekinah of His eternal presence. Two conditions only must be fulfilled: you must be prepared to yield your own will to the cross and to wait before God in the silence and solitude of your spirit.

God was pleased to make this known to Saul of Tarsus. He will be equally pleased to make it known to you because He lives to glorify His Son and to afford the full measure of blessedness to His children. Ask for a breath of heavenly grace to part the veiling mist and show you the line of sunlit Alps irradiate with the morning glow!

CONTACT WITH ANANIAS

It is permitted to holy and humble natures to be a great help to the spirit that is on the point of emerging from bondage. The little maiden, awaking from her death swoon, required food. Lazarus, whom Jesus had called back to life, needed to be unswathed and loosed. The services that one can perform for another are beautifully illustrated in that simple-hearted saint, Ananias, whom the Lord at this moment called upon the scene and to whom He entrusted the keys of the kingdom, that he might unlock Saul's way into perfect peace.

We know very little of Ananias except that he was a devout man according to the law and was well spoken of by the Jews; but evidently he was on intimate terms with his Master. And the Lord was willing to enter into explanations and reassurances with Ananias before sending him forth. A very slender candle, if it has caught the fire, may communicate its glow to the powerful wicks of a lighthouse tower.

Ananias gave Saul a brother's welcome. Though he was fully acquainted with the object of Saul's visit to the city, Ananias approached Saul with the sweet and generous term, *Brother* Saul. What a thrill that address sent through the heart of the new convert! Pharisaism had never spoken this way. And as Saul became conscious of the presence of this new brother standing beside him and laying his hand on his fevered brow, the human love was the sign and symbol of the divine. Ah, love of God, though I have persecuted you so sorely, what must not you be if the love of man be so strong and tender!

He communicated priceless blessings. First beneath the laying on of Ananias's hands, sight came clear to eyes that had beheld nothing since they had been smitten by the glory of "that light." And the touch of this devout man, accompanied as it must have been with the upward glance of prayer and faith, was also the signal for the reception of the anointing grace of the Holy Spirit—infilling, anointing, and equipping for blessed service.

He baptized him. What a baptism must that have been! What a tidal wave of emotion must have swept over Saul as he realized that he was being united with Jesus by the likeness of His death! Years long afterward, the memory of that solemn moment was fresh to him, and he refers to it in the repeated *we* of Romans 6: "So many of us as were baptized into Jesus Christ" (v. 3). "*We* are buried with him" (v. 4). "*We* have been planted together in the likeness of his death" (v. 5). That baptism was Saul's final and irreversible break with his past life, the Pharisaic party, and his persecution of the adherents of "the Way." Henceforth, Saul was avowedly one with the followers of the Nazarene. From that moment, Saul took up his cross and began to follow his Master. The cross and grave of Jesus must now stand between him and all that had been—all his friends, ambitions, and opinions—while he must turn his face toward labor and travail, hunger and thirst, perils and persecutions, together with the daily deliverance unto death for Jesus' sake.

There was an even deeper thought. He knew that the root of sins was sin, the assertion of I, the body of the flesh. Too long had this been the motivating force of his career. His efforts after righteousness, as well as his zeal against the Church, had manifested the intensity and virulence of this strong, selfish principle. Henceforth, however, he desired to be dead to it and to accept the position offered to him in the risen Lord, wherein the body of sin should be done away as the center and impulse of his being because it has been replaced by the indwelling Spirit of Life, which is in Christ Jesus.

> Yea, thro' life, death, thro' sorrow and thro' sinning,
> He shall suffice me, for He hath sufficed;
> Christ is the end, for Christ is the beginning,
> Christ the beginning, for the end is Christ.

It does not appear that Ananias was aware of all that baptism meant to his new brother Saul. To him it was an act of obedience, a symbol of the washing away of sins. This simple soul had never trodden the difficult way of the cross. How little do we know what is passing in the thoughts of those next to us in life's strange school! But Ananias's honest help must have been very comforting to the new disciple as he united himself with the cross of Jesus and henceforth began to fill up that which was behind of the sufferings of Christ for His Body's sake. All Ananias knew was that the Lord had said, "I will shew him how great things he must *suffer* for my name's sake" (Acts 9:16).

THE EDUCATION OF THE DESERT SOLITUDES

"Immediately I conferred not with flesh and blood: Neither

went I up to Jerusalem to them which were apostles before me; but I went away into Arabia" (Gal. 1:16–17). It is not quite clear whether Paul began to preach before going. Probably not. He wanted to be alone, to reflect on all that he had seen, and to coordinate, if possible, the new with the old, the present with the past. For this he must have uninterrupted solitude, and he hungered for the isolation of the wilderness. Men like Ananias might reassure him; the apostles of the Lord might communicate much of his teaching and wondrous ministry; the holy beauty of the life of the infant Church might calm and elevate his spirit; but above all things, he wanted to be alone with Jesus, to know Him and the power of His resurrection, the anointing that makes human teaching needless because it teaches all things. Three years under such instruction would doubtless make him so proficient that when afterward he met those who were of repute among the apostles, they would be able to add nothing to him (Gal. 2:6).

Arabia probably stands for the Sinaitic peninsula, with its sparse population, its marked physical features, and its associations with Moses and the Exodus and Elijah. How much it must have all meant to that eager spirit, who was to interpret for all time the inner meaning of the momentous events of which those gaunt mountain solitudes had been the scene! Here the bush had burned with the fire that now burnt within Paul's heart. Here Moses had seen God face to face, as Paul had seen Jesus. Here the plan of the tabernacle had been communicated, as to Paul that of the Church. Here the water flowed from the stricken rock, and that Rock was Christ. Here Elijah stood in the entrance to the cave, and the still small voice stole into his heart; and had Paul not heard that same voice? Beneath those heavens glowing at noon with sultry heat and radiant at night with myriads of stars, the cloud had moved, directing the march of the pilgrim hosts—for Paul, too, it shone. Month after month, Paul wandered to and fro, now sharing the rough fare of some Essene community or the lot of a family of Bedouins, now swept upward in heavenly fellowship and again plunged into profound meditation. The chariots of God are twenty thousand, even thousands upon thousands, and they were all waiting at his beck and call to bear him aloft into the heavenly places.

Probably the most important work of those years was to review the entire course of Old Testament truth from the new standpoint of vision suggested by the sufferings and death of the Messiah. There was no doubt that He had been crucified in weakness and now lived in the power of God. But how was this consistent with the anticipations of the prophets and seers of the Old Testament who had been understood by generations of rabbis to predict an all-victorious Prince? How eagerly Paul turned to all the well-known Messianic passages! What ecstasy must have thrilled him as he discovered that they were all consistent with Christ's suffering unto death as the way to enter His glory! And how greatly he must have wondered that he and all his people had been so blind to the obvious meaning of the inspired Word (2 Cor. 3).

We can easily understand how, on his return to Damascus, Paul should immediately proclaim that Jesus was the Son of God, and that he should especially confound the Jews who lived there, proving that this is the Messiah. In those silent meditations over the Word, Paul stored arguments for use in many a synagogue for the next twenty years, where he would reason from the Scriptures, opening and alleging that the Messiah must suffer and rise again from the dead and "that this Jesus is the Messiah."

It is almost certain also that Paul was led at this time to understand the relation of the law to the older covenant into which God had entered with Abraham. Up to this moment, Paul had been a son of the law, laboriously fulfilling its demands but groaning beneath a perpetual sense of failure and condemnation. Now he was led to see that he and all his people had made too little of the promise made to Abraham which was conditioned not on works but on faith. To use his own words, he realized that the law, which came four hundred and thirty years after the giving of the covenant, could not disannul it so as to make the promise ineffective (Gal. 3:17). Paul graduated backward from Moses to Abraham. From the loftier summits of Mamre, he beheld the temporary and limited ministry of the law, which, he pointed out, was added "because of transgressions, till the seed should come to whom the promise was made" (Gal 3:19).

In the light of this revelation, Paul could better understand his own call to minister to the Gentiles, for this was one of the special provisions of the Abrahamic covenant: "in thee shall all families of the earth be blessed" (Gen. 12:3).

But deeper than all was God's work with Paul's soul. Grain by grain, Paul's proud self-reliance and impetuosity were worn away. As it happened to Moses during the forty years of shepherd life, so it befell Saul of Tarsus. No longer confident in himself, he was henceforth more than content to be the slave of Jesus Christ—going where he was sent, doing as he was bidden, and serving as the instrument of God's will. We all need to go to Arabia to learn lessons like these. The Lord Himself was led up into the wilderness. And in one form or another, every soul that has done a great work in the world has passed through similar periods of obscurity, suffering, disappointment, or solitude.

7

Acts 22:17–21

THE EMERGENCE
OF THE LIFE PURPOSE

Ah! Fragments of a whole, ordained to be
Points in the life I waited. What are ye
But roundels of a ladder, which appeared
Awhile the very platform it was reared
To lift me on?

Browning

*I*t is a matter of great interest to a mother to watch
the unfolding character of her child from the apparent shapeless-
ness of infancy to the defined outlines of marked individuality. But
it is still more interesting to trace the successive stages of the emer-
gence of the life purpose of a newborn soul. At the moment of conversion, two questions arise naturally upon our lips: first, who are
You, Lord? and next, what will You have me do? *As to the first,* we
can only await the gradual revelation as when the dawn slowly
breaks on a widespread landscape. It will take an eternity to know
all that Jesus Christ is and can be to His own. *As to the second,* we
are no less dependent on the divine revealing hand, indicating the
path we are to tread, showing the scheme that the divine mind has
conceived.

Often at the beginning of the new life we attempt to forecast the work that we hope to accomplish. We take into account our desires and aptitudes, our faculties and talents, our birth and circumstances. From these we infer that we shall probably succeed best along a certain line of useful activity. But as the moments lengthen into years, it becomes apparent that the door of opportunity is closing in that direction. It is a bitter disappointment. We refuse to believe that the hindrances to the fulfillment of our cherished hopes can be permanent. Patience, we cry, will conquer every difficulty. The entrance may be narrow, but surely it is passable. At last we shall reach the wide and large place of successful achievement. We cast ourselves against the closing door, as sea birds on the illuminated glass of the lighthouse tower, to fall dazed and bewildered to the ground. And it is only after such a period of disappointment that we come to perceive that God's ways are not as our ways, nor are His thoughts as our thoughts, and that He has other work for us to do for which He has been preparing us, though we knew it not. When we are young, we strengthen ourselves and attempt to walk where we desire, but in later years we are guided by Another and taken where we would not have gone on our own.

There is a marvelously appropriate illustration of these facts of common experience in the life story that we are considering. Without doubt, at the beginning of his Christian career, the apostle felt strongly drawn to minister to his own people. He was a Hebrew and the son of Hebrews. The pure blood of the chosen race flowed through his heart, nourishing it with the great memories of the past. What was the meaning of his having been cradled and nourished in the heart of Judaism, except that he might better understand and win Jews? Did not his training in the strictest sect of their religion and at the feet of Gamaliel give him a special claim on those who held "that jewel of the law" in special reverence and honor?

But Paul was destined to discover that his newfound Master had other purposes for his life and that he had been specially prepared and called to preach *among the Gentiles* the unsearchable riches of Christ and make *all men* see the fellowship of the mystery that from all generations had been hid in God. How this discovery was made to him is an interesting study because, though at the moment of his arrest it was clearly announced by the Lord Himself that he was to be sent to the Gentiles, yet apparently it did not dawn on his mind then to how large an extent his energies and time would be monopolized by ministering to those who were, at that time, "aliens from the commonwealth of Israel, and strangers from the covenants of promise, having no hope, and without God in the world" (Eph. 2:12).

PAUL'S CHERISHED HOPE

During his sojourn in the Sinaitic peninsula, we may well believe that Paul's soul turned toward his people with ardent desire. Was Paul not an Israelite, of the seed of Abraham, of the tribe of Benjamin? And could he be indifferent to the needs of his brethren according to the flesh? Surely it would not be difficult to unfold the meaning of the sacred symbolism through which their forefathers had been disciplined in those very desolate places. That the rock was Christ, that the water that flowed over the sands foreshadowed Paul's mission to the world, that the law given from Sinai had been fulfilled and reedited in the holy life of Jesus of Nazareth, that the sacrifices offered on those sands had pointed to the death of the cross, and that the fire that burned in the bush had also shone on his face—to teach all this and much more and to lead his people from the desert wastes of Pharisaism to the heavenly places of which Canaan was the type were the hope and longing of his heart. What work could be more congenial to his desires and attitudes than this?

On his return to Damascus, Paul at once commenced his crusade in the synagogues. "Straightway," we are told, "he preached Christ in the synagogues, that he is the Son of God. But all that heard him were amazed.... But Saul increased the more in strength, and confounded the Jews which dwelt at Damascus, proving that this is the very Christ" (Acts 9:20–22). How encouraged he was by these early successes! How evidently God seemed to be setting His seal and imprimatur on Paul's decisions! Visions of national repentance and conversion passed across his eager soul, and Paul dared to hope that he should live to see the dry bones become a great army for God.

But the vision was soon overcast. So violent was the hatred with which Paul was regarded by his fellow countrymen that he was in imminent danger of his life. They seem to have instigated the governor, who held the city of Damascus with a garrison, to assist them with patrols. The gates were watched day and night that he might be killed if he tried to escape. And finally he was lowered under the cover of the night by a basket over the city wall (Acts 9:25).

Still, however, his purpose was unchanged. Paul went up to Jerusalem with the intention of seeing Peter. But in this he would probably have failed had it not been for the intervention of Barnabas, who, according to an old tradition, had been his fellow student, educated with himself at the feet of Gamaliel. Through the help of Barnabas, Paul was brought into contact with Peter and James and was, not improbably, received into the house of Mary, the mother of Mark, and sister to the good Cypriote (Col. 4:10). A blessed fortnight followed. Paul was with them, "coming in and going out at Jerusalem" (Acts 9:28), and especially engaged in holy and loving fellowship with Peter, the acknowledged leader of the Church.

It is surely an innocent use of the imagination to think of Peter and Paul sitting or walking together on the housetop, when the sun was setting, conversing of the great past. On one occasion, their theme would be the Lord's early ministry in Galilee, so closely associated with Peter's opening manhood; on another, the discourses and scenes of the last hours before His crucifixion; on another, the precious death and burial, the glorious resurrection and ascension, and the appearances of the forty days. "Tell me all you can remember of the Master" would be the frequent inquiry of the new disciple of him who had been so specially privileged as a witness of that mystery of love. And it must often have come to pass that as they fellowshipped and prayed together of all those things that had happened, Jesus Himself drew near, and their hearts burned within them.

What Peter could not tell him, James could, for James had shared the home of Nazareth but had remained unbelieving till the resurrection convinced him. He would recount the story of the early years and corroborate Peter's narrative of events from the Easter dawn to the Day of Pentecost.

But Paul had other business in those happy days. He seems to have avoided the churches of Judea that were in Christ and to have again sought the synagogues. "He spake...and disputed against the Grecians" (Acts 9:29). On many a spot where he had contended against Stephen, Paul stood now to contend for the truths that he had first heard from the martyr's life. How well he could understand the passion with which his statements were received, but how skillfully would he drive home the stake that had at last compelled his own surrender! But here also his efforts were met by rebuffs: "they went about to slay him" (Acts 9:29).

Yet in spite of the coldness and antipathy, Paul clung tenaciously to his cherished purpose. He had great sorrow and unceasing pain in his heart; he could have wished himself accursed from Christ for his brethren's sake, his kinsmen according to the flesh (Rom. 9:3). And when he knelt quietly in the temple and heard authoritatively from the Master's lips that Jerusalem would not receive his testimony, he could hardly believe it and clung to his hope, pleading against the idea that the door was closing in his face. "Surely," he cried, "it cannot be that Jerusalem will refuse my words! She has such ample proof of my sincerity. She must be willing at least to listen to the arguments that I have found so compelling. Surely my marvelous change must arrest and impress her. Let me stay. To transfer me elsewhere would be a serious waste of power. I shall do better work here among people who know me so well and conditions I can understand than would be possible anywhere else in the world."

In a similar manner we have all cherished our life purposes. We have forecast our future as likely to lie in a certain direction and have dearly desired that it should do so. When hindrances have been put in our way and when we have met with strong opposition and rebuff, we have still clung to our hope. Only very slowly have we yielded and accepted the inevitable. To renounce it has been like tearing out our heart. Not till long years have passed have we realized that the Lord's plan was so much wiser and grander than our own. Then suddenly we have awakened to discover that while we were desiring to do one thing, God was leading us to do another and that what we have counted secondary was primary, for His glory, and the lasting satisfaction of our own heart.

THE CLOSING DOOR

The door began to close at Damascus. It closed still further when persecution arose at Jerusalem. But the final act was as Paul was praying in the temple (Acts 22:17). It would appear that Paul had gone there to be alone, away from the many voices that were endeavoring to counsel him. For though he had been but a few days in the city, antipathy against him had already risen to such a height that his life was in danger. It was necessary to consider seriously what to do—should he stay or go? should he brave the storm or flee before it? Some advised one course, and some another. The babble of voices confused him, deafening the whisper of the still small voice. Paul's attention was too distracted by human suggestions to be perfectly open to the direction of the finger of God. So he went to the temple, where his Master had so often been, where so many symbols spoke of Him, where holy associations gathered like troops of white-robed angels. And, as Paul knelt in prayer in some quiet spot, he saw Him, whom his soul loved and sought.

How many visit the temple without seeing Him! But if we see Him, we are oblivious to all beside. There is One who is greater than the temple. And the risen Lord gave clear and unmistakable directions, as He always will to those who can say with the psalmist: "My soul, wait thou only upon God; for my expectation is from him" (Ps. 62:5). "[I] saw him saying unto me, Make haste, and get thee quickly out of Jerusalem: for they will not receive of thy testimony concerning me" (Acts 22:18).

It is easy to explain why Jerusalem would not accept Paul's testimony. There was too much of the cross in it. Paul had discovered aspects of the death of Jesus that were in keen antagonism to all that was revered by Pharisaism. It was sufficiently mortifying to their pride to learn that the son of the carpenter was the long-anticipated Messiah, but to be told further that the true spiritual life could be entered only by union with that supreme act of self-renunciation was intolerable. This aspect of Christianity is now too little appreciated, and so the offense of the cross has largely ceased. But wherever it is consistently advocated and practiced, it is certain to arouse the sharpest controversy.

Paul, as we have seen, did not willingly accept this as the ultimatum and still argued that Jerusalem would afford the most suitable sphere for his ministry. It is a mistake to argue with God, as though to bend Him to our will. "Woe unto him that striveth with his Maker! Let the potsherd strive with the potsherds of the earth" (Isa. 45:9). But all debate was at least summarily closed by the words, "Depart: for I will send thee far hence unto the Gentiles" (Acts 22:21).

Ah, Paul! You have argued and strived and tried to have your way. You have almost demanded that the Lord should adopt your views and been adamant against believing that they may not hold. You have knocked vehemently against the closed doors; but it is of no avail. The Lord loves you too much to yield. Someday you will come to see that He was doing better for you than you knew and that He was sending you into yet a wider and more productive sphere of service.

THE OPENED DOOR

So the disciples brought the hunted preacher down to Caesarea and sent him to Tarsus (Acts 9:30). Paul probably resumed his tent-making there, content to await the Lord's will and bidding. But the years passed slowly. Possibly four or five were spent in comparative obscurity and neglect. That he worked for Christ in the immediate vicinity of his home is almost certain, as we shall see, but the word of the Lord awaited fulfillment.

At last one day, as he waited, he heard a voice saying in the doorway, "Does Saul live here?" And in another moment, the familiar face of his old college friend was peering in on him with a glad smile of recognition. Then the story was told of the marvelous outbreak of God's work in Antioch, of the overflowing blessing and the breaking nets, and Barnabas pleaded with him to return to help him gather in the ripening harvest of the first great Gentile city that the gospel had moved. "And when he had found him, he brought him unto Antioch. And it came to pass, that a whole year they assembled themselves with the church, and taught much people" (Acts 11:26).

Be not afraid to trust God completely. As you go down the long corridor, you may find that He has preceded you and locked many doors that you would have entered in vain. But be sure that beyond these there is one that He has left unlocked. Open it and enter, and you will find yourself face to face with a bend of the river of opportunity, broader and deeper than anything you had dared to imagine in your sunniest dreams. Launch forth on it, for it leads to the open sea.

8

ALWAYS LED
IN TRIUMPH

Christ! I am Christ's! and let that name suffice you;
Ay, and for me He greatly hath sufficed;
So, with no winning words I would entice you;
Paul has no honour and no friend but Christ.

F.W.H. Myers

While Paul was waiting in Tarsus, where he remained some four or five years, he appears to have concentrated his energies in the direction suggested by two references in Acts 15. In the twenty-third verse, the apostles and elder brethren address their circular letter expressly to the brethren who are of the Gentiles in Antioch, Syria, and Cilicia. And in the forty-first verse, we learn that Paul, with Silas as his fellow traveler, went through Syria and Cilicia, confirming the churches. Evidently there were infant churches scattered throughout Paul's native province, and the conclusion is almost irresistible that they were born into existence beneath the fervid appeals and devoted labors of the new disciple.

Perhaps at this time Paul's kinsmen, Andronicus and Junia, Jason, Sosipater, and others, were brought to Christ (Rom. 16:7, 21).

But Paul's father, deeply mortified at the blasting of his hopes by the conversion of his son from the old faith, cast him off (Phil. 3:8).

Paul's work, however, was chiefly concerned with the synagogues, which, since the Dispersion, had been established in most of the large cities of the Roman empire. As with the earliest churches in Judea, the main constituents of the synagogues would be converted Jews and proselytes. It is doubtful whether the apostle would have felt himself justified in receiving the Gentiles, as such, into the Church. He was feeling his way in that direction and was being prepared for the full acceptance of the commission with which he had been entrusted on the way to Damascus and when worshiping in the temple.

It has been supposed that some of his deep experiences of privation and peril must have taken place in the course of his efforts to spread the gospel during these years. We read of that marvelous enumeration—labors more abundant, stripes above measure, prisons more frequent, deaths oft, five times the forty stripes save one; thrice beaten with rods, once stoned, thrice shipwrecked, a night and day in the deep; in perils, labor, travail, watching, hunger and thirst, cold and nakedness (2 Cor. 11:23–27). There is positively no room in his life, as narrated by the chronicler of the Acts of the Apostles, for many of these, especially when we call to mind that the second epistle to Corinth was written before Paul's expulsion from Ephesus and therefore before the long series of trials with which the book of the Acts closes. It is, therefore, more than probable that we are to conclude that from the very hour that he began to follow the Savior he became identified with His sorrowful progress through the world: hated, resisted, despised, and crucified, but pursuing his triumphant progress to His throne.

This thought was closely associated in the apostle's mind with his unprecedented experiences, as will appear to any thoughtful student of the second epistle to the Corinthians. Mark especially the second chapter and the fourteenth and fifteenth verses: "Now thanks be unto God, which always causeth us to triumph in Christ, and maketh manifest the savour of his knowledge by us in every place. For we are unto God a sweet savour of Christ, in them that are saved, and in them that perish."

THE METAPHOR

Paul's metaphor was gathered from the scene of a Roman triumph, one of the most notable events in the old world, when some great general—a Caesar or Marius—returning from distant scenes of triumph, ascended the Capitoline Hill amid the plaudits of the assembled citizens and the fragrance of sweet odors. Before his chariot were paraded captive kings and princes; after it came long lines of prisoners laden with the spoils of war. About this time, Claudius was celebrating his victories in Britain, and among his captive princes marched the brave Caractacus.

To the vivid imagination of the apostle—always more prone to use metaphors borrowed from the life of men in camps and cities than from scenes of natural beauty—it seemed as though the pageantry of the scene that so often stirred Rome to its hearts was an appropriate emblem of the progress of Christ through the world: Hades and death bound to His chariot wheels, His arms filled with spoils, His trains composed of thousands whom He had conquered and among whom Paul was proud to count himself.

Is not this an apt picture of every age? Each great crisis in the past has helped to advance the glorious reign of Christ. Was the fall of Babylon a crisis? It gave mankind a universal speech—the language spoken by Alexander and his soldiers—the delicate, subtle Greek in which the New Testament was written. Was the fall of Rome a crisis? It opened the way to the rise of the northern nations that have become the home of liberty and the gospel. Was the fall of feudalism in the French Revolution a crisis? It made the splendid achievements of the nineteenth century possible. And we may look without dismay on events that cast a shadow on our hearts. They also shall serve the cause of the gospel. In ways we cannot tell, they shall prepare for the triumph of our King. Through the throes of the present travail the new heavens and earth shall be born. The agony is not as the expiring groan of the dying gladiator but as the sigh of the mother bringing forth her firstborn. These things, said our Lord, must be, and they are the beginning of travail (Matt. 24:8). And amid all, Jesus rides the triumph to His destined glory and the crown of all the earth.

PAUL'S POSITION

The apostle's personal position in his Master's processing was clearly apprehended and perpetually accentuated. Paul never wearied of describing himself as *the slave of Jesus Christ:* "Paul, a servant of Jesus Christ, called to be an apostle, separated unto the gospel of God" (Rom. 1:1). He had been a rebel chieftain. With fire and sword he had ravaged the flock of God. He had measured his strength with Jesus of Nazareth but had met more than his match. The Stronger One had come upon him, taken away his armor, and bound him with fetters from which he could not get free. He would not if he could, nor could he if he would. From that hour in which he had been dashed to the ground on the road to Damascus, he had been content to be led from city to city, from continent to continent, in the triumphal progress of his Lord, a trophy of His mighty power to bring the most stubborn under His yoke. "Thanks be to God," he cries, "who always leads us in triumph."

Is this how you view your life? Captured! Apprehended by Jesus Christ! Set apart for God! Do you realize that you are bound by the most sacred chains to your Conqueror and are following His chariot through the earth? Life would take on a new meaning if you realized this—that all you are in your person and own in your property is Emmanuel's.

Those whom Jesus leads in triumph share His triumph. They may be a spectacle to angels or to men. Sometimes in the stocks; often accounted the off-scouring of all things; yet, in the spiritual realm, they are made to triumph always. Conquered, they conquer; enslaved, they are free; last in this world but in the front rank of heavenly society. Poor, beaten, vanquished soul, lift up your head and rejoice, for if you are conquered by Jesus, you shall be always made to triumph!

THE INFLUENCE OF CHRIST

The influence of Christ on the character of those who follow Him is also clearly delineated. The metaphor is changed, and the apostle sees himself no longer a slave but a freed servant, a citizen, a friend bearing a bowl of incense from which redolent vapors steal into the air. God makes manifest through him in every place the sweet smell of the knowledge of Jesus. Wherever Paul went, men knew Jesus better; the loveliness of the Master's character became more apparent. Men became aware of a subtle fragrance, poured upon the air, that attracted them to the Man of Nazareth. The world became purer, the tone of society healthier, the morals and manners of men more refined.

What an ideal this is for us all—so to live that though we are unable to speak much or occupy a commanding position, yet from our lives a holy fragrance may be spread abroad that will be not ours but Christ's! Let us live so near Him that we may absorb His fragrance and then go forth to exhale it again in pureness, in knowledge, in long-suffering, in kindness, in the Holy Spirit, in love unfeigned, in the word of truth, and in the power of God. Just as a piece of clay or sponge may become so impregnated with some aromatic spice that it will scent the drawer, cupboard, or box in which it lies, so we may become impregnated with the sweetness of Jesus and spread it by an irresistible influence in every place where we are called to live or work.

WONDERS NEVER CEASING

Yet once again the thought changes. The apostle imagines himself to be no longer the hand that swings the incense bowl but the incense itself. He says, "We are unto God a sweet savour of Christ" (2 Cor. 2:15). How marvelously scent awakens memory! In a moment it will waft us back through long years to some old country lane, garden, or orange grove, summoning to mind people and events associated with it in the happy past.

When, therefore, we are told that we may be to God a sweet fragrance of Christ, it must be meant that we may so live as to recall to the mind of God what Jesus was in His mortal career. It is as though, as God watches us from day to day, He should see Jesus in us and be reminded (speaking after the manner of men) of that blessed life that was offered as an offering and a sacrifice to God for sweet-smelling savor.

What a test for daily living! Is my life fragrant of Jesus? Do I remind the Father of the blessed Lord? Does He detect Jesus in my walk and speech? Is there in me the sweet savor of that daily burnt offering, that delight in God's will, that holy joy in suffering for His glory, that absorption in His purposes that made the life of the Son of Man so well pleasing to God?

At the foot of the Capitoline Hill, the ancient triumph divided. Some of the captives were led off to the dark precincts of the Tullianum, where they were put to death. Others were reserved to live. The same fragrance was associated with the perishing on the one hand and the saved on the other. Thus it is in all gospel preaching and holy living. The sun that melts wax also hardens clay; the light that bleaches linen tans the hands that expose it; the cloud is light to Israel and darkness to Egypt. Those who have spiritual life are helped to intenser life, and those who lack it are only driven to further excesses of sin. To one we are the savor of life unto life, to the other of death unto death.

It was in such a mood that Saul of Tarsus spent the years of preparation that preceded the great opportunity of his life. It was in the cultivation of such virtues that he awaited the coming of Barnabas.

9

Romans 11:13

THE APOSTLE
OF THE GENTILES

*He looked abroad, and spake of some bright dawn
Of happiness and freedom, peace and love;
Day long desired, and now about to break
On all the nations.*

Trench

It is probable that during his years of quiet work in Cilicia and Syria, Saul of Tarsus was being led with increasing clearness to apprehend God's purpose in his life—that he should be the apostle of the Gentiles. The heavenly voices at the commencement of his Christian career had announced that he would be sent to them (Acts 26:17). Ananias had been informed that Paul was to be a chosen vessel to bear the name of Jesus before the Gentiles and kings (Acts 9:15). The vision in the temple had culminated in the words, "Depart: for I will send thee far hence unto the Gentiles" (Acts 22:21). And there is no doubt that the pressing needs of his labor for so many years, amid populations largely composed of Gentiles, made him feel the impulse of the current that was bearing the whole Church toward a new departure. Up until now, Judaism had been the only door into Christianity; henceforth, the door of faith was to stand wide open to Gentiles also, without circumcision. Some suggestion of this is furnished by Paul's own lips: "[I] shewed first unto them of Damascus, and at Jerusalem...and *then to the Gentiles,* that they should repent and turn to God, and do works meet for repentance" (Acts 26:20). But still the true channel bed of his life was hardly discovered until circumstances transpired that now demand our notice.

SUMMONED TO ANTIOCH

Halfway through Luke's narrative, the center of interest shifts from the Mother Church at Jerusalem to one that had been founded shortly before the time we are describing, in the frivolous, busy, beautiful city of Antioch. Connected with the commerce of the Western world by the River Orontes, which flowed majestically through the marble palaces and crowded wharves that lined its banks, and communicating with the thoughtful conservative East by the caravans that brought the merchandise of Mesopotamia and Arabia through the passes of the Lebanon, Antioch was an emporium of trade, a meeting place of the Old World and the New, "an Oriental Rome, in which all the forms of the civilized life of the empire found some representation." It is forever famous in Christian annals because a number of unordained and unnamed disciples, fleeing from Jerusalem in the face of Saul's persecution, dared to preach the gospel to Greeks and to gather the converts into a church in entire disregard of the initial rite of Judaism. There, also, the disciples of "the Way" were first called Christians from the holy name that was constantly on the lips of teachers and the taught. But the imposition of that name shows that the people of Antioch were aware that a new body or sect was in process of formation. From Antioch issued the first missionary expedition for the evangelization of the world. In post-apostolic days, Antioch was famous as the home of the great bishop, saint, and martyr, Ignatius.

The population of Antioch was a rabble of all races, but the Greek element predominated with its licentious rites, its vivacious, sparkling intellect, its marvelously elegant and subtle tongue, its passion for the theater, the arena, and the racecourse. There was need indeed that the river of Life should find its way into that swamp of beautiful but deadly corruption. But it is probable that none of the leaders of the Church would have dared to take the initial step of conducting its streams thus. Peter and the Church at Jerusalem were only just learning, through amazing incidents in the house of Cornelius, that God was prepared to grant to Gentile proselytes repentance unto life. It was left, therefore, to a handful of fugitive Hellenistic Jews, men of Cyprus and Cyrene, to break through the barriers of the centuries and begin preaching the Lord Jesus to the Greeks at Antioch. Instantly, the divine Spirit honored their word and gave testimony to the word of God's grace, and a great number believed and turned to the Lord (Acts 11:19–21).

As soon as tidings of these novel proceedings reached Jerusalem, the Church dispatched Barnabas, who was himself a Cypriote, to make inquiries and report. His verdict was definite and reassuring. He had no hesitation in affirming that it was a definite work of God's grace. He rejoiced that these simple souls had been thrust into so ripe and plentiful a harvest, and he carried on the work that had been inaugurated with such success that "much people was added unto the Lord" (Acts 11:24).

His success, however, only added to the perplexity and difficulty of the situation, and Barnabas found himself face to face with a great problem. The Gentiles were pressing into the Church and taking their places on an equality with Jews at the Lord's Supper and love feasts—an action that the more conservative Jews greatly resented. The single-hearted man was hardly able to cope with the problem. But Barnabas remembered that at Paul's conversion, his old friend and fellow student had been specially commissioned to preach to the Gentiles. And hoping that Paul might be ready with a solution, he departed to Tarsus to seek Paul, and having found him, he brought him to Antioch. "And it came to pass, that a whole year they assembled themselves with the church, and taught much people" (Acts 11:26).

But this year's experience at Antioch was of the utmost consequence to Paul, who learned from Barnabas the conclusion to which the Church at Jerusalem, on hearing Peter's recital of God's dealings with Cornelius and his household, had come (Acts 11:4–18). Paul noticed how evidently the Spirit of God set His seal upon appeals, whether by himself or others, addressed directly to the Gentiles, and thus was led with that deep appreciation that comes from the education of circumstances to see that believing Gentiles were fellow members of the Church and fellow heirs of the promises. God made no distinctions; why should *he*? All the while his horizon was broadening, his confidence increasing, his conception of God's purposes deepening, and Paul was formulating the gospel that he afterward preached among them (Gal. 2:2).

We need not dwell upon Paul's brief visit to Jerusalem at the end of his year's ministry at Antioch to carry, with Barnabas, alms from the Gentile Christians to their suffering Jewish brethren (Acts 11:29–30). Suffice it to say that it established a precedent that Paul followed in later life and proved that there was no sort of antagonism between the new society and the old, but that all were one in Christ. On this occasion, Paul does not seem to have met the apostles, who probably had withdrawn from Jerusalem to avoid the murderous hate of Herod (Acts 12). The gift of the Church at Antioch was, therefore, left with the elders and the Mother Church (Acts 11:30). And nothing occurred to divert the heart of the future apostle from the resolves that were crystallizing with increasing clearness before him.

SET APART BY THE HOLY SPIRIT

It was a momentous hour in the history of the Church when, on the return of Barnabas and Paul from Jerusalem, they met with three others for a season of fasting and prayer. What was the immediate reason for this special session we cannot say, but it is significant that the three prophets and two teachers represented between them five different countries. Were they yearning after their own people and desiring to offer them the gospel, as they now saw they might offer it, apart from the entanglements and restraints of Judaism? We cannot tell. That, however, was the birth hour of modern missions. The Holy Ghost, Christ's Vicar, the Director and Administrator of the Church, bade the little group set apart two out of their number to a mission that He would unfold to them as they dared to step out in obedience to His command (Acts 13:2).

There was no hesitation or delay. The Church set them free from their duties, and the Holy Spirit sent them forth. And that journey was a complete answer to all the questions by which they had been perplexed.

They went first to Cyprus, because Barnabas was connected with it through his birth and estate. Although they proclaimed the

Word of God from one end to the other in the synagogues of the Jews, they had no fruit till the Roman governor called them before him and sought to hear their message, on hearing which he believed (Acts 13:12).

After landing on the mainland of Asia Minor, Paul, contrary to the judgment of John Mark, struck up from the seacoast to the far-reaching tablelands of the interior, four thousand feet above the sea level, with the evident intention of establishing churches on the great trade route that ran through Asia Minor from Tarsus to Ephesus. What might be the result for East and West if this great mutual bridge were to become a highway for the feet of the Son of God! But there the same experience awaited him.

The Jews in Antioch and Pisidia refused, while the Gentiles welcomed them. Indeed Paul was compelled to turn publicly from his own countrymen and hold up the gospel as light and salvation to those whom the prophet described as at the uttermost ends of the earth (Acts 13:47). Then it was that the Word of the Lord spread throughout all the region.

At Iconium, where they fled before a persecution that made it unsafe to remain in Antioch, they again found the malice of the Jews so persistent that they were driven forth into the Gentile cities and district of Lycaonia, where there were probably no synagogues at all. There, too, they preached the gospel and made many disciples (Acts 14:21–22).

Everywhere it was the Jewish element that was obstructive and implacable, while the Gentiles, when left to themselves, received them and their message with open arms. God gave manifest testimony to the word of His grace whenever they unfolded the open door of faith to the Gentiles and granted signs and wonders to be wrought of His servants' hands (Acts 14:3, 27; 15:12).

As Paul quietly studied these indications of God's will, he needed no angel to tell him that as Israel would not hear, God was provoking them to jealousy by them who were not a people. He saw that the original branches were being broken off, that the wild olive grafts might take their place. Blindness was happening to Israel, until the fullness of the Gentiles had been gathered in (Rom. 11:8, 17, 25). Paul's love was not abated. How could it be? Were they not his brethren, his kinsmen according to the flesh? But he must follow the divine plan.

F.B. Meyer

Probably Paul's greatest experience of this journey was his first visit to the warmhearted Galatians, whose country is probably referred to in the vague allusion of Acts 14:24. In any case, his insistence in his epistle that he had preached to them the gospel as he had received it direct and undiluted from Christ compels us to locate his first acquaintance with them at this time and before that memorable visit to Jerusalem to which we shall refer presently and during which he consulted the apostles concerning the gospel he proclaimed (Acts 15; Gal. 2). It is probable that he was detained among them by a painful attack of a persistent malady, aggravated by climatic changes or malaria. "Ye know," Paul says, "how through infirmity of the flesh I preached the gospel unto you at the first. And my temptation which was in my flesh ye despised not, nor rejected" (Gal. 4:13–14). So far from their rejecting him on this account, his sorrows and afflictions only touched them more to the heart and bound them to him. "I bear you record," he says, "that, if it had been possible, ye would have plucked out your own eyes, and have given them to me" (Gal. 4:15).

Paul's success among this affectionate people was remarkable, and it still further deepened the impression that was becoming the guiding star of his career—that he must bend his strength to the salvation of the Gentiles, whose cause had been laid on his heart at the hour of his conversion.

His Apostleship
Recognized By The Apostles

We do not propose to add anything to the biblical discussion in which so much has been urged on either side as to the time when the visit to Jerusalem (referred to in Galatians 2) took place. After carefully considering the arguments of those who would identify it with the visit to bring alms mentioned above and of those who would make it a separate visit for the special purpose of obtaining the opinion of the leaders on his ministry, I fall back on the more generally received view that Galatians 2 refers to the visit mentioned in Acts 15, when, as we shall see in a succeeding chapter, Paul was sent as a deputation from Antioch to Jerusalem to obtain the views of the apostles on the admission of Gentiles into the Church.

It is sufficient for our present purpose to notice that Paul definitely sought the opinion of those in repute among the apostles concerning his teaching, "lest by any means [he] should run, or had run, in vain" (Gal. 2:2). In the course of several interviews, it became increasingly evident to James, Peter, and John that their former persecutor had received a divine commission to the Gentiles. They realized that Paul had been entrusted with the gospel of the uncircumcision (Gal. 2:7). Peter especially recognized that He who wrought in himself unto the apostleship of the Jew was equally energetic in this fervid soul unto the Gentile. The responsible leaders of the Mother Church could not help perceiving the grace that was given to him, and finally they gave to him the right hand of fellowship, that he should go to the Gentiles while they went to the circumcision.

This was the further and final confirmation of the purpose that had been forming in Paul's heart. Paul recognized that he was appointed as a herald and an apostle, a teacher of the Gentiles in faith and truth. He gloried in this ministry and often spoke of the grace that had been given to him, the least of all saints, to preach unto the Gentiles the unsearchable riches of Christ. He never failed to begin his work in any place by an honest endeavor to save some of his own fellow Jews, but he always realized that his supreme stewardship was to those "who are called Uncircumcision by that which is called the Circumcision in the flesh made by hands" (Eph. 2:11).

By the hand of the risen Jesus, Paul had been appointed to the apostleship. In nothing did he come behind the very chiefest of the apostles, and truly the signs of an apostle were accomplished through his ministry in all signs and wonders and mighty works (1 Cor. 9:1; 15:9; Gal. 1:1). Surely, then, it is befitting that the church that bears his name should stand in the heart of the greatest Gentile city of the age and bear the emblem of the death of Christ above its smoke and turmoil—the sign of the work and service of the great apostle of the Gentiles.

10

2 Corinthians 12:2–5

FOURTEEN YEARS AGO

We are not free
To say we see not, for the glory comes
Nightly and daily, like the flowing sea;
His lustre pierceth through the midnight glooms;
And, at prime hour, behold! He follows me
With golden shadows to my secret rooms!

C.T. Turner

*I*f we count back fourteen years from the writing of these words in Second Corinthians, we shall find ourselves amid the events narrated in the thirteenth and fourteenth chapters of the book of the Acts. It was the momentous hour in the history of Christianity when five men, representing five different countries, met together to fast and pray about the state of the world and their duty with respect to it. The evangelist tells us in two chapters the results of that conference, in the separation and sending forth of the two missionaries, and of the hardships, difficulties, and sufferings through which they fulfilled their high calling. But Paul draws aside the veil from his heart and shows us what his inner experiences were during those wonderful months. He was a man in Christ, caught up into Paradise, the third heaven, to hear unspeakable words (2 Cor. 12:4). Luke dwells on the outside; Paul on the inside. Luke speaks of the man; Paul of the man in Christ. Luke depicts the sorrows and tears that beset him; Paul the elation and joy that bore him to the very bosom of Christ so that many pains and sorrows were actually necessary as a thorn, lest he should be exalted above measure on account of the abundance of revelations afforded him (2 Cor. 12:7).

How little we know of one another's lives! Only the little circle around us or some loved one, and sometimes not these, realizes the visions and revelations or hears the unspeakable words that fall to the lot of the favored soul. Perhaps even Barnabas, who shared the toils and perils of this man of God, had little or no conception of what his companion was experiencing. He beheld the same scenes on which their outward gaze rested but not the visions that were unfolded to the inner eye. He heard the voices that sounded in their ears, of blaspheming and reviling critics, with which so few notes of comfort and encouragement blended; but Barnabas was not aware of the still small voice of Christ that bade Paul have no fear.

It would be sad if all our life could be summed up in our journeyings to and fro on life's thoroughfares, our business engagements, or our happy fellowship with the dear ones of the home circle—if there were nothing except what a Barnabas might share and a Luke record. A Chinese picture that lacks light and shade and depth is not art. We need to dwell deep, to have a life beneath a life, to have windows in our heart that look across the river into the unseen and eternal. The pictures that fascinate are those that suggest more than they reveal, in which the blue distance fades into the heavens and the light mist veils mountain, moorland, and sea. Oh, for the peace that passes understanding, the joy that is unspeakable and full of glory, the deep things that eye has not seen, nor ear heard, nor the heart of man conceived! We may be thankful, therefore, that we can supplement the narrative of Luke by the words of the apostle as he recalls what happened to him fourteen years before he wrote.

HOW THE APOSTLE DESCRIBES HIMSELF

A man in Christ, but that did not make him less a man. There are three qualities in a truly manly character: *resolution, fortitude,* and *courage.*

Resolution—that a man will take up one high ambition and aim, pursuing it through good and evil report, through sun and storm. How evidently this characterized the apostle, who pursued his purpose of ministering to the Gentiles from Antioch to Iconium and then to Lystra and Derbe. The hatred of the Jews did not dissuade; the fickleness of the crowds did not daunt; the hailstone storm of stones at Lystra did not turn him aside. It was Paul's persistent ambition to preach the gospel where Christ had not been named so that they should see to whom no tidings of Him had come and they who had not heard should understand.

Fortitude—that a man should be able to sustain sorrow and heartrending anguish. Every true man needs this, for there is no one without his hours of heartrending grief when it seems as though the heartstrings must break and the lifeblood be shed. Then to be strong, to steer straight onward, to dare to praise God, to sit alone and keep silence because He has laid it upon us, to put our mouths in the dust, if so be there may be hope—here is fortitude indeed. But Paul manifested this also when he bore with uncomplaining nobility the cowardice of Mark and the relentless hatred of his fellow countrymen and, after his stoning at Lystra, aroused from what had seemed to be his death swoon, struggled back into the city from which he had been dragged to all appearance a corpse and, having saluted the brethren and specially the young Timothy, started on the following morning to continue his loved work in the neighboring cities of Lycaonia.

Courage—that a man should have a heart like John Knox, the inscription on whose tomb tells us that one lies beneath who never feared the face of clay. Paul never lacked courage. He never flinched from facing an amphitheater full of raging fanatics or braving consuls and procurators or withstanding an apostle who deserved to be blamed (Gal. 2:14). And his heroic courage was conspicuously manifested in this very journey, that instead of taking an easier and more direct route home by way of his native city and the Cilician Gates, he dared to retrace his steps to each of the cities in which he had preached, "Confirming the souls of the disciples, and exhorting them to continue in the faith, and that we must through much tribulation enter into the kingdom of God" (Acts 14:22). At great personal risk, Paul stayed long enough in each place to appoint elders in the infant communities and to pray with fasting, commending them to God, on whom they believed.

When we become Christians, we do not forfeit these characteristics. No, but they become purified of ingredients that might spoil and corrupt them. Apart from Christ, resolution may become obstinacy; fortitude, stoicism; and courage, fatalism. These are exaggerations, and therefore defects. Directly, however, a man is in Christ—not only in Christ for position but also in Christ for condition, not only in Christ for standing but also in Christ in his daily walk, not only in Christ as before God but also in Christ for the surrounding atmosphere of his daily life—then all danger of exaggeration is done away, and the native strength of character is invigorated from the Lion of the tribe of Judah and sweetened by the meekness and gentleness of the Lamb who was slain.

TO SUCH, BRIDAL MOMENTS COME

Days of the bridal of heaven and earth—high days—hours of vision and ecstasy—when the tide runs high and fast and the cup of life brims to overflow. "I knew a man in Christ...caught up to the third heaven...into paradise, and heard unspeakable words, which it is not lawful for a man to utter. Of such an one will I glory" (2 Cor. 12:2, 4-5).

At first we might suppose that the apostle was really describing the experience of someone else. He appears to distinguish between himself and that blessed man whose experience he was describing: "of myself I will not glory, but in mine infirmities" (2 Cor. 12:5). But as this story proceeds and he tells us that by reason of the visions and revelations granted to him there was danger of his being exalted overmuch, it becomes clear that Paul is describing some radiant experiences through which he passed during that first missionary tour—so marked, so blessed, so full of transfiguring glory that their light had not entirely died from his heart though a chasm of fourteen years lay between.

Such experiences may come in hours of great pain. It has been suggested that this rapture into Paradise took place during the apostle's stoning at Lystra. But be this as it may, Paul could find no words to tell what he saw and heard. The disciple whom Jesus loved had a similar experience. He too saw through heaven's open door, but with all his wealth of language, he had failed to do more than ransack creation and revelation for imagery and symbols that leave us in a condition of bewilderment. Paradise would indeed be a poor place if words could describe it. The third heaven would not be worthy of its Maker if its glories did not transcend our furthest imaginings. He hath set eternity in our heart, a capacity for the infinite, a yearning after the divine. In hours of reverie, when stirred by certain notes in music, especially of the violin or organ, when under the spell of a sunset on a summer's eve, when we wake up to love, we know that words are but the tokens of thought, the signs and symbols of realities, and not the realities. Translate into words for me the sighings of the wind through the forest and the withdrawal of the sea down a pebbly beach and the string of sunlight playing on the hyacinth-strewn grass. You cannot! Then you know why the apostle described his experiences in Paradise as unspeakable.

But these hours are as fading as they are unspeakable. Why? *Lest* we should be exalted above measure and become proud. If the apostle feared this, much more should we. *Lest* we should come to trust in an experience as an aim or object of life instead of regarding it as God's seal and testimony that He may withhold if we make more of it than we ought. We must live not in an experience but in Jesus, from whom, as from the sun, all lovely and helpful experiences emanate. *Lest* we should get out of touch with men and women around us, the majority of whom do not live on mountaintops but reside in valleys, where demons possess and worry the afflicted.

Through God's wise providence, such radiant hours do not linger, because our strength is not fed from them. We shall not get much working strength out of whipped cream, however pleasant it tastes; and if we rely only on the raptures of Paradise for our sources of spiritual power, we shall come lamentably short of our true reinforcements. So God, in His mercy, gives them once or twice, now and again, and, at the time of sending them, accompanies them with a thorn that we may be reminded of our utter weakness and helplessness and be driven to avail ourselves of His grace, in which alone is our sufficiency.

Do not expect the vision of Paradise to linger; it would dazzle you and make life unnatural and unreal. Do not regret the passage of the blessed, rapturous hours, light of step and fleet of pace. Do not think that you have fallen from grace when their flush and glow are over. Whether they come to you constantly or not, or even if they never visit you, you are still in Christ, still joined to the Lord, still accepted in the Beloved; and neither height of rapture nor depth of depression shall ever separate you from the love of God that is in Jesus Christ our Lord. Be content, then, to turn, as Jesus did, from the rapture of Paradise, presented on the Transfiguration Mount, to take the way of the cross through which you will become able to open Paradise to souls in despair, like the dying thief.

THE DISCIPLINE OF PAIN

We need not attempt a discussion of what was the nature of Paul's thorn in the flesh. It is of no importance to our consideration here. Enough that it was very painful. Paul calls it "a thorn," as though he were impaled, and it must have been physical, as he could not have prayed thrice for the removal of a moral taint and been refused. In infinite wisdom, God permitted the messenger of Satan to buffet his servant, and all through that first missionary journey, Paul had to face a long succession of buffetings. There were perils of robbers, of waters, of mountain passes, and of violent crowds; but in addition to all, there was the lacerating thorn.

Paul could have suffered from weak eyes or some distressing form of ophthalmia. We infer this from the eagerness of his Galatian converts to give him their eyes, from his dependence on an amanuensis, and from the clumsy letters with which he wrote the postscripts to his epistles (Gal. 6:11). And if this were the case, the pain would be greatly aggravated as he faced the keen blasts that swept the mountain plateau on which the Pisidian Antioch was situated.

Was it during this journey that Paul sought the Lord on three separate occasions for deliverance and received the assurance that though the thorn were left, more than sufficient grace would be given (2 Cor. 12:9)? If so, like a peal of bells, at Antioch, Iconium, Derbe, and Lystra, he must have heard the music of those tender words: My grace is sufficient, *sufficient*, SUFFICIENT for you! Sufficient when friends forsake and foes pursue; sufficient to make you strong against a raging synagogue or a shower of stones; sufficient for excessive labors of body and conflicts of soul; sufficient to enable you to do as much work, and even more, than if the body were perfectly whole—for my strength is made perfect only amid the conditions of mortal weakness.

In estimating the greatness of a man's lifework, it is fair to take into consideration the difficulties under which the man has accomplished it. And how greatly does our appreciation of the apostle rise when we remember that he was incessantly in pain. Instead, however, of sitting down in despair and pleading physical infirmity as his excuse for doing nothing, he bravely claimed the grace that waited within and did greater work through God's enabling power than he could have done through his own had it been unhindered by his weakness.

Ah, afflicted ones, your disabilities were meant to unite with God's enablings, your weakness to mate His power. Do not sit down before that mistaken marriage, that uncongenial business, that unfortunate partnership, that physical weakness, that hesitancy of speech, that disfigurement of face, as though it must necessarily maim and conquer you. God's grace is at hand—sufficient—and at its best when human weakness is most profound. Appropriate it and learn that those who wait on God are stronger in their weakness than the sons of men in their stoutest health and vigor.

11

THE CONFLICT
OF PAUL'S LIFE

Some law there needs be, other than the law
Of our own wills; happy is he who finds
A law wherein his spirit is left free.
...I will not bend again
My spirit to a yoke that is not Christ's.

H. Hamilton King

*I*n the separation of Abraham from country, kindred, and father's house, the story of his people was foreshadowed. As Balaam, under the inspiration of the Almighty, said, "Lo, the people shall dwell alone, and shall not be reckoned among the nations" (Num. 23:9). Their dress, rites, customs, and religious habits were carefully and expressly determined to accentuate their separation, that being withdrawn from the influence of surrounding nations, they might be fitted to receive, keep, and transmit the knowledge of God. In no other way could they have borne the precious deposit entrusted to them down the centuries and maintained their unbroken witness to the unity, spirituality, and holiness of God. Not otherwise could they have become the religious poets, prophets, and teachers of mankind.

The laws of separation were so rigid that Peter did not hesitate to remind Cornelius and his friends of the risk he ran in crossing the threshold of a Gentile's house, although his host was a man of high rank, of irreproachable character, and well reported of by all the nation of the Jews. And when Peter came up to Jerusalem, even his fellow believers who were of the circumcision found grievous fault with him: "[They] contended with him, saying, Thou wentest in to men uncircumcised, and didst eat with them" (Acts 11:2–3). The law of commandments, contained in ordinances, some of them ordained through Moses and many superadded by successive generations of doctors and rabbis, stood like a middle wall of partition between Jew and Gentile.

All these barriers and restrictions were represented in the initial act of Judaism, the rite of circumcision, the importance of which had been magnified to a most preposterous extent. It was affirmed by one rabbi that but for circumcision, heaven and earth could not exist. Another rabbi declared that it was equivalent to all the commandments of the law. It was counted more desirable for a Gentile to submit to this rite than to obey all the affirmative precepts of Moses or to love God and his neighbor. It was supposed that Adam, Noah, Jacob, Joseph, Moses, and Balaam had all been born circumcised and that subsequently the rite was under the special and peculiar charge of the great prophet Elijah, who was always at hand to see to its due observance.

The rigor of these observances was heavy enough in Jerusalem. But in foreign parts, amid great Gentile communities with whom the Jews were constantly engaged in commerce, it became customary to relax the stringency of the bonds of Judaism though always maintaining circumcision, the intermarriage of Jew with Jew, and that particular method of preparing animal flesh for food that is still popular among Jews. It was clear, therefore, that any innovation that Christianity might introduce into Judaism would be more likely to reveal itself at a distance from Jerusalem, where it would not be instantly repressed by the unbending conservative sentiment so strongly entrenched in the metropolis of the national faith. We are not surprised, therefore, that Antioch became the scene of that forward movement led by Barnabas and Paul that consisted in openly welcoming Gentile converts into the Christian community without insisting on their previous conformity to the venerable rite of circumcision.

This marked a great advance. Until then, especially in Judea, the Christians were regarded by the people as a Jewish sect, and so long as they were prepared to attend the temple services, conform to the regulations, and maintain the institutions of Judaism, their belief in Jesus as the long-promised Messiah was regarded as a peculiarity that might be condoned and winked at. It was permissible that they should meet in the love feast so long as they did not forsake the temple; they might pray to Jesus as God if they acted in all other respects as devout Jews. But if this rule had been universally maintained, Christianity, like a stream in a marshy land, would have speedily been lost to view. After a few brief years, it would have been indistinguishable. And Judaism, with its intolerable burden and exaggerations, would have stood forth among men as the only representative of the purest faith that had ever visited our world. The world of the Gentiles would have been hopelessly alienated; the coming of the Kingdom of God would have been put back for centuries even if it had ever emerged from the stifling conditions of its cradle.

All this, however, was prevented by the policy to which Barnabas and Paul had been led. In the epistle to the Galatians (2:4,12), we have a pleasant glimpse of the liberty that the converts in Antioch had in Christ Jesus. Those who were circumcised and uncircumcised joined in the common exercises of Christian fellowship. They ate together without question, and even Peter, when on a visit to Antioch, was so charmed with the godly simplicity and beauty of their communion that he joined freely with them and partook of their love feasts and common meals.

The conservative party in the Jerusalem church, however, on hearing these tidings, was ill at ease. They saw that if this principle were allowed to be universal, it would undermine their authority and eventually rend their religious supremacy from their grasp. They could not tolerate the thought that circumcision might fall into disuse and that the deep spiritual teaching of Moses might become common coin for the handling of Gentile fingers. Therefore, as the first step, they sent down false brethren who were secretly brought in to spy out the liberty that the church at Antioch practiced. Then, when they were assured of the facts, certain men came down from Judea and taught the brethren, saying, "Except ye be circumcised after the manner of Moses, ye cannot be saved" (Acts 15:1).

It was an important crisis and led to the breaking out of a controversy that embittered many succeeding years in the apostle's life. But it also led to some of his noblest epistles and to his exposition of the principles of the gospel with unrivaled clearness and beauty.

GREAT QUESTIONS WERE AT STAKE

This question, for instance: whether Christianity was to be a sect of Judaism, a chamber in the temple, a bud confined in his green sheath, a dwarfed and stunted babe in swaddling clothes that was forbidden its natural development. And this: whether the Levitical institutions of rites and ceremonies, of feasts and fasts, were of a piece with the great moral code of Sinai and Deuteronomy or might be regarded as temporary and liable to change, brought in for a specific purpose but to be laid aside when that purpose was fulfilled. But this most of all: what were the conditions on which men might be saved?

The conditions of salvation are debated in the language of every age. The terms vary, but the controversy is always the same. Substitute Ritualism for Judaism and the rites of the Church for circumcision, and you are confronted by the same questions and issues as were encountered by our apostle. Still men say, "Unless you are christened, confirmed, and received into our church, you cannot be saved." And it is from Paul's store of arguments, with which apparently before his old age his adversaries were silenced, that we must find our weapons as Martin Luther found them before us.

Salvation is not secured by obedience to a rite, by the observance of a code of rules, or even by obedience to a creed that is pronounced orthodox. A man may be precise in all of these and yet be under the wrath of God and his character be scarred by passion and self-indulgence. The only condition of salvation is faith, which believes in Him who justifies the ungodly and receives into the heart the very nature of Jesus to become the power of the new life. How infinitely unimportant, then, compared with faith, is any outward rite. It may have its place as the outward sign and seal of the covenant, but it has no efficacy apart from the spiritual act.

But there is a constant tendency in the human heart to magnify the importance of the outward rite to the minimizing of the value of the spiritual attribute which it should express or accompany. The outward is so much more accessible, manageable, and computable; the spiritual so removed from human vision and manipulation. In these days, men are prone to magnify the ordinances of baptism and the Lord's Supper in the precise manner in which these Judaizing Christians magnified circumcision. And when they are allowed to do so, their whole theory of religion becomes mechanical and formal. Those who punctiliously follow their precepts are hopelessly led into the ditch, while those who denounce their error are denounced and consigned to the uncovenanted mercies of God.

Let us never forget, then, that "in Jesus Christ neither circumcision availeth anything, nor uncircumcision; but faith which worketh by love" (Gal. 5:6), a new creature, and the keeping of the commandments of God. And let us never fail to follow the example of the apostle, who said, "To whom we gave place by subjection, no, not for an hour; that the truth of the gospel might continue with you" (Gal. 2:5).

THE ARGUMENTS ON EITHER SIDE

"When therefore Paul and Barnabas had no small dissension and disputation with them" (Acts 15:2).

Did not Jesus fulfill the law of Moses? Was He not circumcised? And did He not rigorously observe the temple fasts and feasts, and even pay His share in the temple tax?

Certainly, said Barnabas and Paul. But you must remember that when He died He said, "It is finished," and the veil of the temple was rent from the top to the bottom to show that Judaism had finished its God-given mission. From that moment, He became not only the Savior of Jews but also the world's Redeemer. When God ratified the new covenant with the blood of Calvary, He made the first covenant old. "Now that which decayeth and waxeth old is ready to vanish away" (Heb. 8:13).

But surely the law given by Moses is permanent. Did not Jesus of Nazareth assert that not one jot or tittle should pass away until all was fulfilled?

Precisely. But surely we must distinguish between the outward and inward, the ritual and ethical, the form and the substance. It is impossible to believe that the sublime ceremonial of Leviticus, which was imposed for a special purpose, can be of the same binding force as the ten words of the law that are borne witness to by the conscience of all men.

But if you do away with the restrictions of the law, will you not loosen all moral restraining and lead to a general relaxation of all bonds in the family and the state?

There is no fear of this, the stalwart defenders of the simplicities of the faith answer from the other side. Souls that are united to Jesus Christ by faith are cleansed by receiving from Him tides of spiritual life and health so that they become more than ever pure and holy and divine. Do we then make the law of none effect through faith? God forbid; no, we establish the law. The righteousness of the law is fulfilled in us, who walk not after the flesh but after the Spirit. The law of the Spirit of life in Christ Jesus makes us free from the law of sin and death (Rom. 8:2–4).

THE APPEAL TO JERUSALEM

The disputing and questioning, however, showed no signs of abating, and it was finally decided that Paul and Barnabas and certain others with them should go up to Jerusalem to consult the apostles and elders about this question. They traveled slowly through Phoenicia and Samaria, declaring the conversion of the Gentiles in each of the little Christian communities on their route, until they reached Jerusalem, where, in a great missionary convocation specially convened, they told all the things that God had done with them—that it is in cooperation and fellowship with them, as though by blessing them the living Christ were Himself implicated in the methods they had adopted. But their statements were interrupted by the uprising of certain of the sect of the Pharisees who believed and the heated interjection of the reiterated statement, "It was needful to circumcise them, and to command them to keep the law of Moses" (Acts 15:5).

Again a special meeting was summoned in which there was much questioning. Then Peter arose and said, "This matter was settled in my judgment by God Himself, when in the house of Cornelius the Holy Spirit descended on uncircumcised Gentiles as on us at the beginning. If He made no distinction, why should we?"

Next Barnabas and Paul repeated their wondrous story, this time laying emphasis on the fact that they were only the instruments through whom God worked and showing how greatly the Gentiles had been blessed and were being blessed altogether apart from circumcision.

Finally, James summed up the whole debate by enumerating some three or four minor points, on which he thought it well to insist, for the right ordering of the young communities; but he did not mention circumcision among them, nor did he insist on obedience to the Mosaic and Levitical institutions. To his sage counsel the apostles and elders agreed.

This unanimity between the leading apostles and the two evangelists, who were the cause of the whole controversy, was probably largely due to the private interview that Paul had sought with them and which most commentators allocate to this period (Gal. 2:2). Paul tells us that he went up by revelation as though, in addition to the request of the Church, there were strong spiritual pressure exerted on him. And when he reached Jerusalem, he laid before them who were of repute the gospel he was preaching among the Gentiles, lest he were running in vain. But to his great satisfaction, they did not comment adversely upon his statements, nor did they insist upon Titus, a young Greek, being circumcised. Indeed, they even went so far as to recognize that the gospel of the uncircumcision had been entrusted to him, giving him and Barnabas the right hand of fellowship, that they should go unto the Gentiles as themselves unto the circumcision (Gal. 2:9). The power of the risen Jesus was so mighty in His servants that there was no denying their callings.

The Pharisee party was defeated and a decree signed in the sense of James's address, but from that moment a relentless war broke out that followed the apostle for the next ten years of his life and cost him many bitter tears. Every church he planted was visited by the emissaries of his virulent opponents, who were not content with insisting on the necessity of circumcision but who asserted that Paul was no apostle because he had only seen Christ in vision and had never companied with Him during the days of His flesh. They spoke evil of his personal character, misrepresented his reluctance to take the gifts of his converts, dwelt with cruel animosity upon his personal defects, and in many cases succeeded in alienating the love and loyalty of his converts.

This cruel persecution is constantly alluded to in the epistles to the Galatians and Corinthians and cut Paul to the heart. However, Paul never allowed himself to be defeated. By prayers and tears, by arguments and persuasions, by threatenings and expostulations, the heroic lionheart fought the good fight to the end. If we may judge from the tone of his later epistles, Paul was permitted to see the close of the controversy, in which it was determined once for all that the new-wine Christianity should not be poured into the worn-out bottle skins of Judaism.

If the conditions of justification are now clearly defined as repentance toward God and faith in our Lord Jesus Christ, if salvation is as free as the flowers of spring or the air of heaven, if we are able to stand fast in the freedom with which Christ has made us free, if we may preach to all and any that those who believe are justified from all things—it is because of the unflinching courage with which the great apostle of the Gentiles contended for the faith once delivered to the saints and which led him on one occasion to confront even the apostle Peter himself "because he was to be blamed" (Gal. 2:11).

12

Acts 16

A LESSON
OF GUIDANCE

Oh, let thy sacred will
All thy delight in me fulfil!
Let me not think an action mine own way,
But as thy love shall sway,
Resigning up the rudder to thy skill.

Herbert

*A*fter a brief respite, Paul proposed to Barnabas that they should return to visit the brethren in every city where they had proclaimed the Word of the Lord and see how they fared. This was the beginning of his second missionary journey that was to have far-reaching results.

Barnabas suggested that they should take Mark with them as before, a proposition that his companion positively refused to entertain. Mark had deserted them on the threshold of their previous expedition, and there was grave fear that he might do so again. Barnabas was as strong on the other side. Perhaps he felt that he had some rights in the matter, as the senior in age, because of the tie of blood between himself and his sister's son. At last the contention reached so acute a stage that it seems the Church became aware of it and took Paul's side, for the narrative tells us that Paul chose Silas and went forth, "being recommended by the brethren unto the grace of God" (Acts 15:40).

Whenever we are about to undertake some great enterprise for God, in proportion to its importance we may expect to encounter the strong man armed, "straddling across the way." How often he attempts to overthrow us through the emotions or attitudes of our associates! The crew mutinies as Columbus nears the long-looked-for coast! Nothing tests us more than this. It is difficult to be resolute and gentle, strong and sweet. Beware of temptation from this side, fellow workers. If you are compelled to differ from your companions, let it be in love. Let them feel that you have no interests to serve but those of truth. If Lot quarrels with you, it is best to give him his own terms and send him away (Gen. 13). God will give you ever so much more than Lot can take. Only do nothing to drive the Holy Dove of God from your bosom. Perfect love is the only atmosphere in which the divine Spirit can manifest His gracious help.

Through regions rich in flowers and natural beauty, Paul and Silas traversed Syria and Cilicia, confirming the infant churches that probably owed their existence to Paul's earliest efforts. So through the Cilician Gates to Tarsus, Paul's native city. There was no welcome for him there. Probably the old home was either broken up or forever shut against him, and the two companions in travel threaded the steep valley in the mounts behind Tarsus, leading them up to the central plain with its volcanic deposits and biting winds. After some days' toilsome journey, they came to Derbe, Lystra, and Iconium, so dramatically associated with the former journey.

What a welcome Paul would receive! How many inquiries would be made after Barnabas! How much to tell and hear! There was, however, a special burden on the apostle's heart. On the occasion of his previous visit, Paul's attention had been arrested by a mere lad who had been strongly attracted to him, watching with a lad's enthusiastic devotion his teaching, conduct, purpose, faith, long-suffering, love, and patience, and perhaps mingling with the little group that stood around him when he sank beneath the stones of those who a few days before had offered him worship. He asked for Timothy and was glad to learn that he had not been faithless to the teachings and training of the godly women who had watched over his developing character and instructed him in the Holy

Scriptures. It would seem that the whole family was more or less closely associated with the infant church life; so much so that though the mother was a Jewess, she had not urged her son's compliance with the initial Jewish rite. It had therefore remained in suspension, according to the broad and liberal views that Paul inculcated.

All the reports about Timothy were favorable. He was well reported of by the brethren who were at Lystra and Iconium. The more Paul knew of Timothy, the more he was attracted to him, and he finally proposed that Timothy should accompany him on his travels as his own son in the faith (Acts 16:3). Paul administered the rite of circumcision, not because he deemed it obligatory but as a matter of convenience, that there might be no obstacle to the admission of his young assistant to Jewish synagogues.

A simple ordination service was then held in which Timothy was solemnly set apart for his great work. The elders gathered round and laid their hands on his bowed head and prayed. In answer to their believing intercession, he received the gift of sacred speech. Paul, in later years, reminds Timothy to stir up the gift that was in him through the laying on of his own hands and of those of the presbytery (1 Tim. 4:14).

Thus, the Spirit of Jesus led his servant to call new laborers into the harvest field and endow them with special qualifications for their work. It appears, indeed, that Paul had remarkable power in these directions. In his epistle to the Galatians, Paul expressly refers to his having ministered to them the Holy Spirit by faith (Gal. 3:5), and when Paul laid his hands on the twelve disciples at Ephesus, the Holy Spirit came upon them, and they spoke with tongues and prophesied (Acts 19:6). In the old time, it seems to have been possible for men of God to receive for others and transmit spiritual gifts to them by faith, adapting them better for their lifework. But this was altogether distinct from any mechanical communication of sacramental grace and was the peculiar prerogative of those who were themselves richly endued with the Spirit of Jesus.

Leaving Lystra, Paul and his companions visited the churches in the highland region of Phrygia and Galatia, everywhere distributing the letter of James. They next assayed to go into the populous and influential cities of Asia Minor, such as Colossa, Laodicea, and Ephesus. What could they do better than bear the light of the gospel to those teeming multitudes who sat in darkness and the shadow of death? Yet it was not to be: "[they] were forbidden of the Holy Ghost to preach the word in Asia" (Acts 16:6). Eventually Paul would do some of the greatest work of his life in that very region, but just now the door was closed against him by the Holy Spirit. The time was not yet ripe for the attack on these apparently impregnable bastions of the kingdom of Satan. Apollos must come there for pioneer work. Paul and Barnabas are needed yet more urgently elsewhere and must receive further training before undertaking this responsible and arduous task.

The travelers therefore took a northern route with the intention of entering the important province of Bithynia, lying along the shores of the Black Sea. But when they came to a point in the great Roman road, opposite Mysia, and were attempting to go out of Asia Minor into Bithynia, "the Spirit suffered them not" (Acts 16:7).

Checked when they attempted to go to the west, they were now stopped as they sought to go to the northeast. There was nothing for them but to keep straight on until they came out at the terminus of the road on the seacoast, at the famous harbor of Troas, the ancient Troy. There they met with Luke, whose presence is thereafter denoted by the significant personal pronoun *we;* and there the man of Macedonia beckoned the little missionary band across the straits to set up the banner of Christ on the hitherto untouched continent of Europe (Acts 16:9).

What an extremely attractive title that is for the Holy Spirit! He is preeminently the Spirit of Jesus. When Jesus was glorified, He was given in Pentecostal fullness, and the chief aim of His mission and ministry is to glorify the Lord Jesus and gather together the members of His Body, fitting them for union with their Head. He is also the Comforter and Guide of the saints until the Church is presented faultless to her Lord.

It is interesting to study the method of His guidance as it was extended toward these early heralds of the cross. It consisted largely in prohibitions, when they attempted to take another course than the right. When they would turn to the left, to Asia, He prevented them; and when they sought to turn to the right, to Bithynia, again He withheld them. He shut all the doors along their route and bolted them so that they had no alternative but to go straight forward. In the absence of any prohibition, they were left to gather that they were treading the prepared path for which they had been created in Christ Jesus.

GREESON, TERI A

Hold note:

Pickup location:	Tillamook Main
Patron Email:	mrsterigreeson@gmail.com
Patron barcode:	97141000245049
Patron phone:	503 842 8418
Title:	The life of Paul : a servant of Jes Christ / F.B. Meyer ; edited for
Item barcode:	0736701069568
Author:	Meyer, F. B. (Frederick Brotherton), 1847-

Hold Slip

Whenever you are doubtful as to your course, submit your judgment absolutely to the Spirit of God and ask Him to shut against you every door but the right one. Say, "Blessed Spirit, I cast on You the entire responsibility of closing against my steps any and every course that is not of God. Let me hear Your voice behind me whenever I turn to the right hand or the left. Put Your restraint on me. Do not allow me to go my own way."

In the meanwhile, continue along the path that you have been already treading. It lies in front of you; pursue it. Abide in the calling in which you were called. Keep on as you are unless you are clearly told to do something else. Expect to have as clear a door out as you had in. If there is no indication to the contrary, consider the absence of indication to be the indication of God's will that you are on His track.

The Spirit of Jesus waits to be to you, O pilgrim, what He was to Paul. Only be careful to obey His smallest prohibitions, and where, after believing prayer, there are no apparent hindrances, believe that you are on the way everlasting and go forward with enlarged heart. "Teach me to do thy will; for thou art my God: thy spirit is good; lead me into the land of uprightness" (Ps. 143:10). Do not be surprised if the answer comes in closed doors. But when doors are shut right and left, an open road is sure to lead to Troas. There Luke awaits and visions will point the way, where vast opportunities stand open and faithful friends are waiting.

13

Philippians 4:15

YE PHILIPPIANS

These are the tones to brace and cheer
The lonely watcher of the fold,
When nights are dark, and foemen near,
When visions fade, and hearts are cold.

How timely then a comrade's song
Comes floating on the mountain air,
And bids thee yet be bold and strong—
Fancy may die, but Faith is there.

Keble

*F*or a busy, footsore, heart-weary man, misunderstood and misrepresented, pursued by many anxieties and cares, there must be some place where the heated spirit can cool and the soul unbend in the atmosphere of love and on the couch of tender sympathy. Even Jesus needed a Bethany. It is wonderful when this is found within the precincts of home, when the door that shuts out the rush and glare of life shuts us in to love and sympathy and those tender ministries that are the peculiar province of a woman's life. How little does the great world realize the large share that woman's influence has had in nourishing the patience and courage of its noblest heroes! In the privacy of the domestic life will be found those tender hands that wash the stripes, pour in the oil, and enable the soldier again to take the field.

To many, however, of the world's greatest benefactors, though they have stood in profound need of this tender sympathy, the home life has been denied. Theirs has been a solitary and lonely lot, partly because of the pressing needs of their position and partly because it has been difficult to find or reveal themselves to a kindred soul. This was largely the case with Paul. A self-contained, strong, heroic soul, he resembles the lofty mountains of his native Tarsus, whose slopes are clad with rich verdure and vegetation while their summits rear themselves in steep and solitary majesty. Few have been endowed with a tenderer, warmer disposition. The minute and particular greetings with which his epistles close, the rain of hot tears in parting from his friends, his anguish of mind in having hurt those whom he was compelled to admonish and rebuke, his longing for companionship—are evidences of the genuineness and tenacity of his affection. But it was his appointed lot to have no settled dwelling place—no spot he could call home.

> Yes, without cheer of sister or of daughter;
> Yes, without stay of father or of son;
> Lone on the land and homeless on the water,
> Pass I in patience till the work be done.

Yet the apostle had marvelous powers of attracting men and women to himself. We have seen how he threw the mantle of his magnetic influence over Silas and Timothy, and the Galatians were ready to give him their eyes. But he was now to win a group of friends who would never cease to love him while life lasted; whoever else was alienated and weary, they would be true; whatever trouble threatened to engulf him, it would only elicit their more profuse ministrations; and Philippi was to become to him the one bright, sunny spot in all the earth, more than Tarsus that had disowned him, more than Jerusalem that would cast him out, and next to the "far better" of Paradise.

> Hearts I have won of sister or of brother,
> Quick on the earth or hidden in the sod.
> Lo, every heart awaiteth me, another
> Friend in the blameless family of God.

LUKE

The beloved physician seems to have met Paul first at Troas. This could hardly have been by prearrangement, as the apostle found himself, so to speak, forced to take his journey to that ancient seaport, famous for its traditional interest as the scene of the siege of Troy and thriving on its mercantile relations with East and West. All the northern provinces of Asia Minor sent their produce there for shipment to Macedonia and Greece, and there the merchants of the west, men of Macedonia, would bring their freights in exchange. It is conjectured that Luke, himself a native of Philippi, had followed in the wake of commerce to pursue his profession as a physician to his countrymen. Paul's temporary sojourn in the crowded ghetto may have induced a return of the acute disease from which he had suffered in Galatia, or Paul may have been laid low by malarial fever, to deal with which the nearest available physician was summoned, and this was Luke. In any case, here the two men met, and here in all likelihood the servant of God won his medical attendant for the Savior. In the enthusiasm of an ardent attachment, the new disciple elected to become Paul's fellow traveler so as to be able at all times to minister to the much-suffering and frail physical body of his friend's dauntless and vehement spirit.

Luke is immediately taken into the closest confidence. He forms one of the little group to whom one morning Paul tells of the vision of the man of Macedonia, and he helps to formulate the conclusion, in which Silas and Timothy and he agreed, that the apostle's path lay across the blue waters of the Aegean, dancing and sparkling in the morning light. He goes forth to seek passage in one of the many craft that lay at the wharves and records with manifest love of the sea and knowledge of the land the successive stages of their voyage and journey to Philippi.

How dear Luke became to the apostle, and how tenaciously he clung to his charge, is clear from two expressions penned, the one from the hired house of the first Roman imprisonment, the other from the chill prison cell of the second. "Luke, the beloved physician" (Col. 4:14); "only Luke is with me" (2 Tim. 4:11).

LYDIA

Lydia was probably a widow, but it is for certain that she was a woman of considerable business capacity, with energy enough to leave her native city of Thyatira and cross the sea to establish herself in Philippi as agent for the sale of the purple dyed garments for which her native town was famous. Scripture indicates that she disposed of the finest class of wares, and she must have possessed a considerable amount of capital to be able to deal in such expensive articles. She was also an eager seeker after God. The Jewish community at Philippi, being too small and poor to have a synagogue of its own, was obliged to meet by the riverside in an enclosure or garden screened from public observation. But there she was as the Sabbath came round, with members of her household, listening to the Jewish Scriptures and seeking after God, if perhaps she might find Him, not realizing that He was not far from every one of them.

On one memorable Sabbath, when only women were present, four strangers—Jews—appeared in the little circle and "sat down, and spake unto the women which resorted thither" (Acts 16:13). This was the first gospel sermon in Europe. And it is somewhat remarkable that it was addressed to a handful of women in the open air. Lydia was the first of a great succession of holy women who have welcomed the Lord Jesus as their Sovereign and Spouse. And the open air has been the scene of the greatest victories of the cross.

The result of that morning service was Lydia's conversion. Whether she received the apostle's message of the crucified and living Lord at once or gradually is not clear—most likely her heart opened as a gloomy sky opens to the sun. But the result was that she, with her entire household, came over to believe in Jesus, whom Paul preached, and she felt as sure about her own conversion as she was eager for Paul to come and abide in her house: "If ye have judged me to be faithful to the Lord, come into my house, and abide there" (Acts 16:15). It was a blessed change, leading to far-reaching consequences in her own life and in Paul's.

She must have been a woman of considerable determination and perseverance to have overcome Paul's reluctance to be dependent on any of his converts. "What is my reward then?" he asks on one occasion, "that, when I preach the gospel, I may make the gospel of Christ without charge.... It were better for me to die, than that any man should make my glorying void" (1 Cor. 9:18, 15). He would bear anything rather than risk the imputation of the suspicion that he was making profit out of the gospel. Rather than this, he worked day and night that he might be chargeable to none, and with his own hands he ministered to his own necessities and to those who were with him. But Lydia was able to override all his objections—"She constrained us" (Acts 16:15) is Luke's reflection as he reviews the scene. So the four companions in travel found rest and entertainment in her hospitable home.

How much this large-hearted and resolute woman did in later days it is impossible now to decipher from the record of the past. We know of four separate occasions in which the Philippian church sent supplies to their beloved founder and teacher (2 Cor. 11:9; Phil. 4:10–18). And this was very probably due to Lydia's foresight and generosity. No other church performed so large a ministry, because no other church could perform it. As Paul indicates, they were for the most part in deep poverty. And it is probable that the Philippians would have been as paralyzed as the rest had it not been for Lydia and her household, who thrived on the proceeds of their trade. It has even been surmised that Paul owed much of the comfort of later days, when he spent two years in the palace of Caesarea waiting for his trial and two more years in his hired house at Rome, to the same source; and it may have been some inkling of the well-to-do friend who held Paul dear that induced Felix to keep him in bonds (Acts 24:27).

A statement gained credence in the early Church that Paul and Lydia were married, but there is no foundation whatever for this in Scripture, and the probabilities against it are overwhelming. The whole argument of 1 Corinthians 7 and 9 may be adduced to show that the stories of Lydia and Thekla are alike inadmissible. We are rather inclined, therefore, to think of Lydia as a noble, truehearted, and devoted friend of the apostle, who counted it her privilege as well as her joy that he should reap temporal benefits in return for the spiritual blessings that he had so richly sown in her heart. Her reward will be one day to hear from the Master's lips that in making the burdens of His servant lighter, she had been ministering to Him and that having received an apostle in the name of an apostle, she must have an apostle's reward.

MINOR CHARACTERS

Minor characters are cast on the canvas, drawn from life, and filling up the picture: the hysterical girl, demon possessed, who marked and followed the evangelists, designating them slaves of the Most High God, and who proclaimed the way of salvation; the syndicate of owners who fattened on the proceeds of her divination as she showed miners where to find the gold, girls the day to wed, merchants the period to set forth their ventures, and who were correspondingly chagrined when Paul's challenge to the spirit emancipated his wretched victim and ended their hopes of further gain. The Roman magistrates, who strangely forgot the high traditions of their office, were swept off their feet by the urgency of the rabble and, without going through even the formality of a trial, tore clothes off the backs of the accused with their own hands and laid "many stripes upon them," uncondemned, being Romans (Acts 16:22–23). Looking back on the way these petty officials treated him, Paul recalls how much he suffered and how shamefully he was entreated (1 Thess. 2:2). There was also Silas, who well justified Paul's choice of him, for he showed himself well able to bear shame and suffering for Jesus. It was good that Mark was not there! How would he have stood it? But from these our thought turns to the third principal actor in this scene, the story of whose conversion has shed the light of unspeakable comfort into myriads of broken hearts.

THE JAILER

A rough, coarse man, probably! What else could be expected from one who had spent his early days in the Roman army and his later ones amid the hardening and brutalizing experiences of a provincial Roman prison? When superiors did not hesitate to act in defiance of law and decency, their subordinate could hardly be expected to be too particular. Barbarous usage would certainly be meted out by his hands to the two Jews, about whom he had received the significant hint that he was to keep them safely. The inner prison was a dark underground hole beneath his house, and into this he thrust them (Acts 16:24). They would probably lie extended on the bare damp ground, their bleeding backs in contact with the soil and their legs stretched to such an extent by the stocks as to almost dislocate their hips.

By midnight the two prisoners became so happy that they could no longer contain themselves and began to sing, chanting the grand old Hebrew psalms and, in the intervals, praying (Acts 16:25). No doubt they were in the best of company and found their souls overflowing with exuberant joy. "Bless the LORD, O my soul: and all that is within me, bless his holy name" (Ps. 103:1). It was an uncommon sound to the other prisoners, who stood or lay around in the pitch dark, their chains stapled to the walls—not one of them thought of sleep; "the prisoners," we are told, "heard them" (Acts 16:25).

An earthquake broke in on the singing, the doors flew open, and the staples left their places. The jailer, being roused from sleep, came into the prison yard and found the doors open. As Paul and Silas caught sight of him standing against the glimmering starlight, to their horror they saw him draw his sword and prepare to kill himself rather than face an ignominious death for his infidelity to his charge. With a loud voice, Paul called out and reassured him; then the call for the light, the springing into the cell, the trembling limbs, the courtesy that led them out, the inquiry for salvation, the answer of peace, the motley midnight audience that gathered around the two servants of God, the loving tending to their wounds, the baptism, the hastily prepared food, the glad rejoicing of the transformed believer and all his believing house. One event crowding on the heels of another and making a swift, glad series of golden links that bound the jailer ever after to his Savior and to Paul.

Paul doubtless became one of the members of the Philippian church, a community of singular purity and loveliness, to whom the apostle wrote his tenderest words without a syllable of rebuke. He could only thank God upon every remembrance of them, and in every supplication for them, he made request with joy. They were beloved and longed for, his joy and crown. He longed after them all in the tender mercies of Christ Jesus. They were his Bethany, his Zarephath, his well of Bethlehem.

14

Acts 17, 18

FROM PHILIPPI TO ATHENS

Whoso hath felt the Spirit of the Highest
Cannot confound nor doubt Him, nor deny:
Yea, with one voice, O world, tho' thou deniest,
Stand thou on that side, for on this am I.

F.W.H. Myers

THESSALONICA

Leaving Luke at Philippi, Paul and his companions traveled through Amphipolis and Apollonia to Thessalonica, a name that lives forever in the inscriptions of his two earliest epistles. The modern town is known as Saloniki. It may be that Paul was specially attracted to this city because of the synagogue and a weekly Jewish service there, in which he could carry on his favorite work of opening and alleging from the Hebrew Scriptures that the Messiah must suffer and that He had appeared in the person of Jesus of Nazareth. Paul did this for three Sabbath days, maintaining himself and his friends by the work of his own hands and lodging with a man named Jason, who afterward became a devoted disciple and follower (Rom. 16:21).

At the end of that period, the strong feeling raised among the

Jews made it unwise for Paul to continue in the synagogue, so he removed his conferences to some neutral ground. How long he remained there we cannot tell, but it must have been long enough for the formation of a healthy and vigorous church, toward which the apostle bore himself with the gentleness of a nurse and the encouragement of a father. Something about these Macedonian converts was immensely attractive to him. In later years he speaks of them as his joy and crown, and he says that he was so affectionately desirous for their growth in grace that he would gladly have sacrificed his own life to promote it. The people were very poor, and Paul worked day and night with his own hands, even to travail, that he might not be burdensome to them; but they were rich in faith and love and hope (1 Thess. 2:6, 7, 11, 19).

More than in other cases, Paul's teaching led the Thessalonians to anticipate the advent of the Lord. The pressure of the anguish that lay heavily upon them all may have made them peculiarly susceptible to those radiant visions of the Lord's return that filled the apostle's thought. They even outran Paul's teaching and fell into the error of supposing that that day had already come—an error that the apostle by a second epistle hastened to correct. It was a great joy, however, to that harassed heart to realize that amid the furious opposition of man, God was working with him and accompanying his words with the demonstration of His Spirit. Paul recalls with vital satisfaction that the gospel came to them in power and the Holy Ghost, so that they became examples to all who believed in Macedonia and Achaia, and the Word of God sounded forth from them in clarion notes (1 Thess. 4; 2 Thess. 2).

Some months must have been occupied in this blessed ministry. The strain on the apostle was evidently greatly lessened by the gifts that came from Philippi, relieving Paul from the necessity of manual toil (Phil. 4:16).

At last, however, Thessalonica was closed against Paul and his traveling companions. Paul and Silas were compelled to flee by night before the anger of the populace, incited by the Jews. The accusation laid against them was a strange one, considering the quarter from which it emanated. It was suspicious that Jews should be so eager to maintain the integrity of the Roman Empire in opposition to the claims of the other King, one Jesus. But "any stick will do to beat a dog with," and the Jews were not scrupulous about the means they employed as long as they could rid themselves of their powerful rival, who was probably thinning the crowd of Gentile devotees who gathered in their synagogue.

BEREA

Fifty miles of night journey brought the men to Berea, and there for a brief space they had rest, as the Jews were more open-minded and more willing to search the Scriptures to discover for themselves the reasonableness or otherwise of Paul's views. But Paul's heart yearned for the beloved brethren whom he had left to stem the strong tide of hatred that his teaching had evoked. More than once he would have returned had it not been for the fear of implicating Jason and others, who appear to have been bound over to prevent him from setting his foot again in Thessalonica. This was in his mind when he said Satan hindered him (1 Thess. 2:18).

The project of Paul's return to Thessalonica was, however, rendered quite impossible by the rising of another storm, caused by Jewish emissaries from that city who pursued his steps with relentless hate. There was at last no recourse but to leave Silas and Timothy in Berea, to see what further could be done to keep the pathway to the rear open, and to hurry down to the harbor to take the first boat that was sailing, which happened to be headed for Athens. Those who conducted Paul hurried him on board, and we can imagine him standing on deck and watching wistfully the receding heights of Mount Olympus slowly fading from view; *behind*, the dearest, truest friends he had ever known; *before*, what?

ATHENS

The messengers hastened back to Berea, bearing the charge of the lonely lionheart that Silas and Timothy should come to him with all speed. While Paul waited for them and hoped they would assure him that he might return to the infant communities he had founded, he passed through the streets of Athens, surveying the monuments of their religion. On every side were the achievements of human genius. Temples that a Phidias had designed, statues that a Praxiteles had wrought. But Greece was living Greece no more. Her political glory had passed away a century and a half before, when she had fallen before Rome's all-subduing might. She prided herself still on her heroic traditions and her custodianship of the greatest monuments of that or any epoch of human history. But it was the afterglow of sunset.

It is not clear that the heart of the apostle was stirred with classic memories or artistic appreciation. To him the city was simply full of idols, and the innumerable multitudes suggested the confused notions that prevailed of the unity and majesty of the deity. Paul was greatly moved (Acts 17:16), and not content with reasoning in the synagogue with the Jews and proselytes, he went forth every day into the marketplace to reason with whomever he met, urging everyone to turn from these vanities to worship the only God. It was his constant aim to be all things to all men, and at Athens he gave a conspicuous exhibition of his marvelous versatility. No ordinary Jew could have entered so thoroughly into the spirit of the place as did the great apostle or excited sufficient interest among its philosophers to justify their calling a special assembly of the council of the Areopagus to hear a full statement of the new teaching he brought to their ears. The evangelist indicates that the opinions formed about Paul were diverse and not entirely complimentary. Some compared him to a bird picking up seeds, others to a seeker after novelty, and perhaps there was more of hostility than friendliness in their taking hold of him and bringing him before their highest religious tribunal (Acts 17:19).

It was the greatest audience Paul had ever addressed. Before him were philosophers, pedants, lecturers, and students, who were accustomed to discussing the loftiest themes within the horizon of human thought and to making distinctions to which the delicate refinement of the Greek language lent itself with marvelous subtlety. Epicureans were there to taste the flow of words or criticize the style, the choice of images, the harmony of balanced sentences. Stoics were there to study the theory of life that this new theorizer, as he appeared, professed. The whole crowd of Athenians and resident strangers were interested only in saying or hearing something new.

The address Paul gave on that occasion is unique (Acts 17:22–31). For its grace, intellectual sequence, grandeur of conception and range, stately march of eloquent words, it stands alone among the addresses recorded for us by the evangelist. It was probably the result of deep thought and prayer, or Paul would not have so carefully passed it on to Luke, who was not then with him. It reveals the opulence of the apostle's intellect and that power of ready sympathy that enabled him to adapt himself so easily to all sorts and conditions of men.

We can only notice the contrasts between himself and his audience that reveal themselves in almost every sentence. To the men of Athens it was a new sensation, a shift in the kaleidoscope of religious thought; to Paul it was a matter of tremendous urgency, his spirit pressed and provoked within him. They confessed their ignorance of the Unknown God, who lay behind the world and all things therein; Paul withdrew the veil and declared Him unto them. They supposed that the temples around them were not unworthy of the divine abode; he told them, as he remembered Stephen to have said years before, that nothing less than heaven's infinite dome could befit His supernal majesty and that even this could not contain Him. They thought to propitiate the deity with gifts; Paul insisted that He needed nothing at men's hands and that their blessedness consisted in giving not goats and calves but broken hearts, contrite spirits, and empty, outstretched hands. They taught a dreary kind of pantheism, as though God were no longer distinct from the matter of the world; Paul said that He was a person, a Father to be sought after, as well as the atmosphere in which they lived and moved and had their being. It did not seem unbecoming for them to fashion the similitude of the Godhead in gold and silver and stone, graven by art and man's device; but Paul insisted that He was Spirit, to be worshiped in spirit and in truth. Some held the immortality of the soul, as Socrates had proclaimed it on that very spot, but they had no idea of the resurrection of the body; Paul, however, unhesitatingly affirmed that spirit would mate again with body, not only that there would be a literal resurrection but also that there had been one and that a day was coming in which God would judge the world by the Man who died in mortal weakness but whom He had raised from the dead.

At this mention of the resurrection, many in his audience began to mock. The Greek found the perfect fruition and glory of life in the present and had no idea of a future that should involve the reanimation of the body. So Paul departed from among them with comparatively small results. Dionysius, a member of the august tribunal before which he had stood; a woman, Damaris, who was probably the result of his more general work in the city; and a few others joined with Paul and believed. The gospel attracted the simple-minded merchants and artisans of Macedonia more readily than the educated *literati* of Athens.

So far as we know, the apostle never visited Athens again. He went sadly on his way to Corinth, his heart filed with a tumult of thoughts—anxiety for the infant churches behind him, yearning to see Timothy and Luke, questioning what reception he might receive amid the cultured and eloquent Corinthians. But more than ever, Paul determined not to know anything among them save Jesus Christ and Him crucified (1 Cor. 2:2), while steadfastly abjuring all attempts at wisdom or grace of speech lest the cross of Christ should be made void.

15

1 Corinthians 2:3

IN WEAKNESS
AND FEAR

Ay, for this Paul, a scorn and a despising,
Weak as you know him, and the wretch you see—
Even in these eyes shall ye behold him rising,
Strength in infirmities and Christ in me.

F.W.H. Myers

*F*ive hours' sail across the Saronic Bay brought the apostle to Cenchrea, the port of Corinth to the east, for this great and busy city commanded two waterways. Through her western port, Lecheum, she was in communication with the Adriatic, and through her eastern port, Cenchrea, with the Aegean. The wares of the East thus passed through her to supply the omnivorous appetite of the metropolis, and vast crowds were attracted to her precincts for the purposes of trade. This commanding position thus gave her a quite unusual importance in the eye of the apostle, ever eager to seize on any advantage that he could use for the gospel of his Lord. To establish a strong Christian Church there would be to cast seeds of Christian teaching on waters that would bear them east and west. Christian missionaries should be strategists, expending their strength where populations teem and rivers of worldwide influence have their rise.

But the apostle entered the proud and beautiful city "in weakness, and in fear, and in much trembling" (1 Cor. 2:3). He could not forget the frigid contempt that he had encountered in Athens, and that was harder to bear than violent opposition. He may have been suffering from some aggravation of his persistent thorn trouble without Luke's presence to treat it. And he was profoundly conscious of being deficient in those gifts of learning and eloquence of which the Corinthians set such importance. He knew that his speech and his preaching could never be in persuasive words of human wisdom, and it was his fixed determination to know nothing among them but Jesus Christ, and Him crucified (1 Cor. 2:2).

Many other difficulties were to be encountered that made his ministry in Corinth the more difficult and his consequent success the more conspicuous.

THE NECESSITY FOR CONTINUAL MANUAL TOIL

In his first epistle to Corinth, Paul lays great emphasis on his manual labor. Always maintaining the right of those who preached the gospel to live by the gospel, he did not use that right but suffered all things rather than hinder the gospel's progress or influence (1 Cor. 9:12). No chance should be given to the merchants and traders who thronged the city from all parts, prepared to sacrifice everything for purposes of gain, to allege that Paul was prompted by mercenary motives. Paul therefore resumed his trade of tentmaking and was thankful to come across two Christian Jews who had been flung on this shore by the emperor's decree that expelled all Jews from Rome (Acts 18:2). Suetonius, the historian, tells us that this decree was the result of tumults caused by one Chrestus, evidently referring to violent disputes in the Jewish community concerning the claims of Jesus to be the long-expected Messiah. With them, therefore, Paul lived and worked, for they were of the same craft, and a friendship sprang up between Paul and Aquila and his wife Priscilla that was destined to have an important bearing on the spread of Christianity in the metropolis from which the couple had come and in Ephesus, to which they would accompany their newly made friend. Perhaps Paul was employed by them, but in any case, work was hard to find and wages scant, so that he was not infrequently in actual need (2 Cor. 11:9; 1 Cor. 4:11–12).

How strange that the movement that was to give Corinth a greater fame than her games or architecture or eloquence emanated from a poor shop in the Jewish ghetto, where a handful of fugitive Jews worked at their trade, speaking amid their toils of Jesus of Nazareth, who had been crucified in weakness but was living through the power of God. They also were weak with Him, but they were destined to live and reign with Him, over the hearts of men, through the power of God.

THE VIRULENT HATRED OF THE JEWS

According to his usual practice, Paul journeyed to the synagogue every Sabbath and reasoned, persuading the Jews and Greek proselytes that the conception of the Hebrew Scriptures was precisely that of a suffering and crucified Messiah. This went on for some weeks, but the measure of his labors was somewhat curtailed by the heavy drain of his daily toil. It was not till Timothy and Silas arrived, the one from Thessalonica and the other from Berea, bringing cheering news of the steadfastness of his converts and hands filled with generous gifts, that Paul was able to give more time and intensity to the cherished object of his life. "Paul was pressed in the spirit, and testified to the Jews that Jesus was Christ" (Acts 18:5).

This was more than the influential men of the Jewish community could bear. They opposed, blasphemed, and drove Paul from the synagogue. Their attitude was more than usually virulent. They were unreasonable and wicked; they were animated by the spirit that had led their nation to kill the Lord Jesus and the prophets; they pleased not God and were contrary to all men, filling up the measure of their sins (1 Thess. 2:14–16; 2 Thess. 3:2).

Their hatred culminated when the apostle gladly accepted the offer of a God-fearing proselyte—Titus Justus, whose house was close to the synagogue—to hold meetings at his house. This new move was followed by instant and remarkable success. Among those who migrated with the apostle from the synagogue was Crispus, its chief ruler, who believed in the Lord with all his house. Many of the people of Corinth, also, heard, believed, and were baptized. As the new meeting house became more crowded and the movement increased in numbers and influence, the Jews became more and more exasperated and at last rose in a body, seized Paul, and dragged him before the Roman governor, who happened to be Gallio, brother to Seneca, the famous philosopher and Nero's tutor (Acts 18:12). Gallio was a man of unusual culture and refinement, sweetness, and lovableness. He represented the broad and liberal views of educated Romans, of the policy that Rome should exercise toward the various religions of the provinces. When Gallio discovered that the charge against Paul was of no imperial importance and had to do indeed not with facts or civil wrong or moral outrage but with words and names and Jewish law, he would have nothing more to do with it or them, but commanded his magistrants to drive them from the judgment seat (Acts 18:14–16).

The Greeks were only too glad that contempt should be heaped on the hated Jews and took the opportunity of seizing Sosthenes, the new chief ruler of the synagogue who had succeeded to the post vacated by Crispus, and beating him in the very presence of the proconsul. Gallio regarded their horseplay with perfect indifference. What did it matter if a Jew got a few stripes more or less? No doubt it was felt that they were richly merited, and so long as there was no public disturbance, the castigation might serve a useful purpose in cautioning the Jews against bringing their matters into public notice or trespassing on the public patience.

But the incident must have greatly aggravated the hatred of the Jews against the apostle and his converts, especially when, as it would appear, Sosthenes himself became a convert and so intimately associated with the apostle as to be coupled in later years with Paul in the inscription of the first epistle to the Corinthians—"Sosthenes our brother" (1:1).

THE CHARACTER OF HIS CONVERTS

Corinth has been compared to Paris for its vice, to Newmarket for the preponderance of the sporting interest, to Chicago for the mixture of its population, and to Vanity Fair for its frivolity and lightness. The scum of the world gathered there. Soldiers and sailors, slaves and prostitutes, jockeys and chariot drivers, athletes and wrestlers, Romans with their imperial bearing, Greeks with their regular features, Jews with their unmistakable badge, Scythians from the shores of the Black Sea, men of Mesopotamia, Pontus, Egypt, and Asia Minor—all bent on business or amusement and painted to a greater or lesser extent with the exceeding evil of this grossly impure city. The Temple of Venus, with its thousand priestesses, legalized vice; the Isthmian Games, held once in three years, established betting and gambling; the motley character of the population encouraged a wild admixture of thought and opinion, for which there was no recognized standard or court of appeal.

To such a city Paul opened his message, encouraged by the assurance of the Lord that He had much people there (Acts 18:10). How often to His tried and persecuted servants does the Master come as He came to the apostle! They may be conscious of weakness and much fear, may speak His Word in trembling, may be derided as a spectacle and laughingstock, may be encompassed with toil and pain and persecution, but Christ stands beside in a vision and says: "Be not afraid, but speak, and hold not thy peace: for I am with thee, and no man shall set on thee to hurt thee" (Acts 18:9–10). They may gather themselves against you, but their gathering is not sanctioned by God. Whosoever shall gather against you shall fall for your sake. No weapon that is formed against you shall prosper, and every tongue that shall rise in judgment against you shall be condemned.

With this encouragement in his heart, Paul labored with marvelous success for a year and six months in this sinful city. It is true that not many of the wise or mighty or noble of this world were among the chosen ones; they who were accounted by the high-bred leaders of Corinthian society as weak and base and contemptible were selected as the foundation stones of the newly gathered church (1 Cor. 1:26–29). There might be a Crispus and Gaius, a Stephanas and his household, all of whom, contrary to his usual practice, the apostle baptized before Timothy and Silas arrived. But these were exceptions to the general rule. Perhaps women had special influence in the young community, as the apostle devotes so much space in his epistle to regulating their behavior. We know, at least, of Phoebe, the deaconess of the church at Cenchrea who bore his epistle to Rome, and of Chloe, whose household slaves were the messengers of intelligence when Paul was at Ephesus.

The majority of his converts, however, were of the lowest caste and of those who had been deeply stained with the vices that made Corinth notorious. The city was the resort of fornicators, idolaters, adulterers, effeminate, thieves, covetous, drunkards, revilers, and extortioners, and such had they been (1 Cor. 6:9–11). But under the preaching of the cross, in the power of the Holy Ghost, a marvelous change had passed over them—they had become washed, sanctified, and justified in the name of the Lord Jesus and in the Spirit of our God. Jesus had become their wisdom, righteousness, sanctification, and redemption. Delivered from the power of darkness, they had become children of the light and of the day: heirs of God and joint heirs with the Son of His love.

What a contrast between that little church and the great heathen world out of which it had been chosen! We may imagine one of its meetings toward the close of the apostle's visit. It is a Sabbath evening. Outside, the streets are full of pleasure seekers and revelers. Groups of idlers are discussing the last chariot race or staking their money on an approaching boxing match. The varied costumes, vivid gestures, handsome carriages, the mimes and plays, the processions and shows, compose a graphic picture of movement and color. But within the little meeting place, all is hushed and still. Paul is speaking of things that eye has not seen nor ear heard nor the heart of man conceived (1 Cor. 2:9); or the men in turn are contributing to the edification of the rest, with a psalm, or a teaching, or a revelation, or the interpretation of an unknown tongue; while the women, modestly veiled, listen in silence. Now the love feast is being partaken of, each bringing some contribution of food to the common meal, and presently the Lord's Supper will conclude the evening engagements, partaken of according to the method delivered to the apostle by the Lord Jesus Himself (1 Cor. 11, 12).

This was a marvelous sequel to Paul's timid and unadorned entrance among them. But it is evident that the apostle was far from satisfied. He complained that he could not speak to them as spiritual men but as to carnal believers, babes in Christ, and that he was obliged to feed them with milk and not with meat. He doubtless, detected the first working of that unhallowed leaven that was afterward to break out in such fearful ferment. Even before he left, there were probably manifestations of party spirit, of the appraising of gift above grace, of the mistaking license for liberty, of the undue prominence of women in public assembles, of greed in the love feasts, confusion in the ministrations, and heresy in the doctrine of the resurrection. It must have been, therefore, with no small misgiving that he tore himself away at the close of his long stay, leaving the infant community to the care of God with much of the same solicitude with which Moses' mother Jochebed launched the cradle ark on the tawny waters of the Nile.

But though he left the city, it produced an ineffaceable effect upon his methods of thought and expression. It was there that he came under the influence of those imperial conceptions that were embodied in Rome, the undisputed mistress of the world. There he wrote his first two epistles--those to the Thessalonians. There, also, he was compelled to study the intimate questions connected with the formation and government of churches so heterogeneously constituted. And there Paul reached the final form of stating the gospel. Years afterward we find him alluding to the mingling of gold, silver, and precious stones with wood, hay, and stubble in the construction of temples and other buildings, or comparing the body to a temple, or drawing illustrations from the boxing match and the arena, the triumphal procession and the theatrical representation. It seemed as though his speech were dyed with the coloring borrowed from the spectacles with which he had grown so familiar in the streets of Corinth.

At last, however, Paul resolved to leave Corinth. Many reasons prompted this step, among them the desire to proceed to Jerusalem to ascertain the feeling of the Mother Church. Still further to conciliate the conservative element there, he had bound himself in the vow of a Nazarite and was anxious to perform the concluding ceremonial within the temple. He was obliged to have his head shaved at Cenchrea because the month had expired, but he carried the hair with him to be burnt on the great altar within the temple court. Aquila and Priscilla probably thought that Ephesus would be a better market for their wares than Corinth, so they sailed with him. And thus the first memorable missionary tour in Greece came to an end, and for the fourth time since his conversion, the apostle approached the city that was doubly dear to him--memories of his Lord being now entwined with the sacred associations of David, Solomon, Hezekiah, and Ezra.

16

Romans 8:36–37

MORE THAN
A CONQUEROR

Servant of God, well done! Well has thou fought
The better fight, who single hast maintained
Against revolted multitudes the cause
Of Truth—in word mightier than they in arms.

Milton

*T*hese words of our text from Romans 8 are among
the greatest words ever spoken by man and are the more remarkable when we consider them as gathering up and recapitulating the
experiences that immediately preceded their utterance.

It was toward the close of Paul's third missionary journey.
About three years before, he had left the Syrian Antioch for the third
time, after remaining there for some duration (Acts 18:23). His
eager spirit could not rest amid the comparative comfort and ease
of the vigorous church life that was establishing itself there, but
Paul yearned with tender solicitude over his converts throughout
the region of Galatia and Phrygia. He therefore again passed the
Cilician Gates, traversed the bleak tablelands of the upper or highland country, strengthening all the disciples and working toward

the Roman province of Asia, which lay to the southwest on the seaboard. He had been previously forbidden to enter Asia (Acts 16:6), but his steps were now as clearly led to it as they had formerly been restrained. Thus does our Sovereign Lord withhold His servants from the immediate fulfillment of their dreams, that they may return to them again when the time is ripe and they are more thoroughly equipped. The experiences of Paul in Greece were of the utmost possible service in fitting him for his ministry in this thickly populated and highly civilized district. The result was a work of evangelization throughout the neighborhood and in the ultimate formation of those seven churches to which the risen Lord addressed His final messages in Revelation.

It was to redeem a pledge he had solemnly made that the apostle at last came down to Ephesus. He had spent one Sabbath day there previously on his way from Corinth to Jerusalem. On that occasion, his ministering had so deeply interested the Jews that they had urged him to abide for a longer period. But this being impossible on account of the necessity of hastening to Jerusalem to fulfill his vow, Paul said, "I will return again unto you, if God will" (Acts 18:21). It was in fulfillment of that promise that the apostle now visited this metropolis of Asia Minor.

A good deal had happened in the interval, in narrating which the evangelist probably gives us the clue to the former prohibition of the apostle's visit. Apollos, the eloquent Alexandrian, had visited the city and met there Paul's friends Aquila and Priscilla, who were awaiting their fellow worker's return. Through them Apollos had been led into a clear appreciation of the truth, in consequence of which his ministry had become more fruitful, both in helping those who had believed and in powerfully confuting the Jews. The strong ploughshare had turned up the heavy clods and prepared the soil for Paul's further labors (Acts 18:24–28).

But Apollos had now left for Corinth, and Paul arrived to take up and extend the work so auspiciously begun. He probably did not know as he entered Ephesus how long he would remain or realize the far-reaching results of his residence. It was enough for him to know, as he afterward wrote to the Ephesian converts, that there was a prepared path awaiting him. But whether the path would be smooth or rough was known only to Him whose he was and whom he served.

As a matter of fact, it was a conflict from first to last. "I have fought with beasts at Ephesus" (1 Cor. 15:32) was his comment after it was all over. And here, again, in enumerating his experiences, Paul compares them to a battlefield and himself to a combatant, crying: "we are killed all the day long; we are accounted as sheep for the slaughter. Nay, in all these things we are more than conquerors through him that loved us" (Rom. 8:36–37). In these words, written to Rome from Corinth after the close of his work at Ephesus and while his experiences there were yet fresh to his thought, he gives us his own conception of the entire situation.

THE BATTLEFIELD

Several difficulties were to be encountered that must be taken into account if we would estimate the greatness of the victory achieved through the grace of the living Savior.

In the first place, there was the pressure of the strange, eager mass of human beings, whose interests, aims, and methods of thought were so foreign to his own. No one has stood alone in the midst of Benares, India, surrounded by that vast heathen population worshiping on the banks of the brown and muddy Ganges or ascending the thousand stairs of the marble temples that extend along the riverside, without a sense of loneliness and isolation. In the proximity of the great river, among those mighty and ancient pyramids of stone, beneath those facades and colonnades in which swarms the infinite life of India, how insignificant the life of the individual onlooker appears! What is he in the presence of that teeming mass! How can he hope to affect its habits of thought and life—he might as well attempt to divert the course of the ancient stream. Did not Paul feel thus as he spent his first weeks at Ephesus?

Besides, there was the vast system of organized idolatry that centered in the temple of Diana, whose image was said to have fallen from Jupiter (possibly a meteorite) and was enshrined in a temple and counted to be one of the wonders of the world. The magnificence of uncalculated wealth, the masterpieces of human art, the fame of splendid ceremonials, the lavish gifts of emperors and kings, the attendance and service of thousands of priests and priestesses combined to give it an unrivaled eminence of influence and prestige. Sooner might some humble Protestant missionary working in a back street of Rome expect to dim the magnificence of St. Peter's or diminish the attendance of its vast congregations as might Paul hope that his residing in Ephesus could have any effect whatever on the worship of Diana. Moreover, all the world knew that the city of the Ephesians was temple keeper of the great Diana and of the image that fell down from Jupiter (Acts 19:35) and therefore was keen to avenge the least slight.

In connection with the temple, there flourished a great trade in amulets and charms. Each individual in the vast crowds who came up to worship at the shrine was eager to carry back some memento of his visit, and the more so if the keepsake would serve as a preservative against evil omens and spirits, of which there was a great and constant dread. The trade in these articles must have been a large one, or the artificers in silver would not have been numerous enough to fill the city with confusion and to necessitate the interference of the town clerk. We might compare today's trade in alcohol to the business in these miniature shrines manufactured by Demetrius and his fellow craftsmen. How impossible it seemed that one man, in three years, employing only moral and spiritual weapons, could make any difference to this ancient and extensive craft!

Also, like many cities of the time, filled with motley populations—part Oriental and part Greek—Ephesus was deeply infected with the black arts of the exorcist, the magician, and the professor of cabalistic mysteries. The renegade Jews were foremost skilled in such matters, calling mystic names over any who were possessed of evil spirits. Even the converts to Christianity found it hard to divest themselves of their former association with these practices, and they treasured their books to the amount of "fifty thousand pieces of silver" (Acts 19:19). It is no child's play to turn a nation of savages from their confidence in witchcraft and medicine men to sane views of life and divine providence, but how much harder to neutralize such insidious poison as flowed through a great city like Ephesus! After an appeal to the soothsayers and magicians, the people fixed the days of marriage and journeying, the engagements they should make, and the business transactions on which they should enter. It was a formidable task to combat their rooted prejudices and habits.

But perhaps Paul's most inveterate foe was the Jewish synagogue, entrenched in ancient prejudices and persistent disbelief. The Jews were hardened and disobedient, speaking evil of "the Way" before the multitude (Acts 19:9). Paul also recalls in his farewell address to the Ephesian elders the trials that befell him by the plots of the Jews. When the great riot broke out, the Jews were only too glad to show their hatred of the Christians by putting forward Alexander to disavow all connection with them (Acts 19:33).

Such were the giant obstacles that confronted the humble tent-maker as he settled down to his trade in company with Aquila and Priscilla. But he looked far beyond the limits of his workshop to great victories for his Lord, much as Carey, who worked at his cobbling with a map of the world in front of him. But greater was He who was for Paul than all who there were against him, and in all these things, Paul was destined to be more than a conqueror through Him who had loved him.

Let Us Verify This Assertion

Let us turn to the Acts of the apostles and ask whether Paul were indeed more than conqueror. The answer is unmistakable. After three months' conflict with the Jews in their synagogue, the apostle was driven to the course he was accustomed to adopt under similar circumstances—he moved his disciples to the schoolhouse of one named Tyrannus and taught there daily (Acts 19:9). In consequence of these ministrations, "all they which dwelt in Asia heard the word of the Lord Jesus, both Jews and Greeks" (Acts 19:10)—a very strong statement when we bear in mind the populousness of that crowded province. Even the silversmiths who caused the riot acknowledged that not only at Ephesus but also almost throughout all Asia, Paul had persuaded and turned away many people. There was great danger that the temple would be depleted of its worshipers and Diana deposed from her magnificence.

The trade in amulets and charms had fallen off so seriously that the craftsmen realized that unless they took action themselves, their gains would be at an end. In addition, the magicians and exorcists, whose position was strongly entrenched, were utterly baffled and confounded by the much greater miracles that were wrought through Paul (Acts 19:11–12). So powerful were the miracles that the handkerchiefs Paul used to wipe the sweat from his brow and the aprons in which he worked at his trade were made the medium of healing virtue as they were carried from his person to the sick and demon possessed. So mighty was the impression that Christ had secrets superior to the best contained in their ancient books that many of them who had believed came confessing and declaring their deeds. And not a few of those who practiced magical arts brought their books together in one of the open squares and burned them in the sight of all. So mightily grew the word of the Lord and prevailed (Acts 19:19–20).

The exorcist Jews, too, were silenced. It would appear that the name of Jesus, spoken even by those who did not believe in Him, had a potency over evil spirits such as no other name exerted. His name had been blasphemously used by vagabond Jews, who had taken upon themselves to call that sweet and holy name over some who were possessed. But in one notable instance, the demon himself had remonstrated, crying, "Jesus I know, and Paul I know; but who are ye?" and he had leapt on them and mastered them, so that they fled from the house naked and wounded (Acts 19:15–16).

LET US CONSIDER
THE TALISMAN OF VICTORY

If we turn from Paul's outward life to study the diary of this wonderful man who seemed singlehanded in his conflicts and victories, we find a moving record of his sorrows and trials. Writing during these eventful months, Paul speaks of himself as a man doomed to death and made a spectacle to the world; for Christ's sake, a fool, weak and dishonored; suffering hunger and thirst, when work was scant and poorly paid; having no certain dwelling place because unable to hold a situation long together through the plotting of his foes; hated, buffeted, reviled, persecuted, defamed; made as the filth of the world and the offscouring of all things (1 Cor. 4:9–13).

When Paul tells the story of the affliction that came upon him during his residence in Asia, he says that he was weighed down exceedingly beyond his power, so much so that he despaired even of life. He tells us that he was pressed on every side, perplexed, pursued, smitten down, groaning in the tabernacle of his body, and always bearing about the dying of the Lord Jesus. In addition to all these things that were without, there pressed on him daily the care of all the churches. There was also his anxiety about individuals, as he ceased not to admonish every one of them night and day with tears (2 Cor. 1:8; 4:8; 10:27–28).

There is nothing more moving in the records of human suffering and patience than the story of Paul's Ephesian experiences as he summoned the elders of the church upon the shores of Miletus in his parting address to them (Acts 20:18-38). In Romans 8:36, he quotes the old words of the psalmist about being killed all the day long and counted as fit for the slaughter. And he enumerates tribulation, anguish, persecution, famine, nakedness, peril, and sword as ingredients in his cup. Added to this was the constant suffering caused by the thorn in his flesh. As the result of it all, we wonder how such a man under such drawbacks and in the face of such opposing forces could be more than a conqueror. Evidently we are driven to seek the source of his victory outside himself: it was through Him who loved. Not only did Paul overcome, he was more than an overcomer. Paul overcame with ease and brought off the spoils of victory—and this because he was in daily communication with the One who had loved, did love, and would love him, world without end. Christ was ever pouring reinforcements into Paul's soul as divers who are groping for pearls in the depth of the sea pour fresh oxygen in their lungs.

The only matter about which the apostle felt any anxiety was whether anything could occur to cut him off from the living, loving Lord. "Who shall separate us from the love of Christ?" (Rom. 8:35)—that was the only question worth consideration. Taking the extreme conditions of our existence on earth, Paul carefully investigates them, knowing that they include all between. First, he interrogates the extremes of existence: death and life; next, the extremes of created intelligences: angels and principalities and powers; next, the extremes of time: things present and things to come; next, the extremes of space: height and depth; and lastly, the extremes of the created universe: any other creature (Rom. 8:38-39). Each of these extremes has thus passed in review, and Paul has eagerly peered into its depths. Paul is like a man investigating every link of the chain on which he is going to swing out over the abyss. Carefully and fervently he has tested all and is satisfied that none of them can cut him off from the love of God. And since that is so, he is sure that nothing can ever intercept those supplies of the life and strength of God that shall avail to make him more than a conqueror.

We strangely misjudge the love of God. We think that our distresses and sufferings, our sins and failures, may make Him love us less, whereas they will draw Him nearer and make His love exert itself more evidently and tenderly. In the home, it is not the strong, healthy children who so engross the mother's care as much as the disabled child who cannot help itself and reciprocate her love. And in the world, death and pain, disease and sorrow, failure and sin, only draw God nearer, if that be possible. So far from separating from His love, they bind us closer.

O blessed love that comes down to us from the heart of Jesus, the essence of the eternal love of God dwelling there and coming through Jesus to us—nothing can ever stop, nothing exhaust, nothing intercept it! It will not let us go. It leaps the gulf of space without weakenings, it bridges time unexhausted. It does not depend on our reciprocation or response. It is not our love that holds God but God's love that holds us. Not our love to Him, but His love to us. And since nothing can separate us from the love of God, He will go on loving us forever and pouring into us the entire fullness of His life and glory. Whatever our difficulties, whatever our weakness and infirmity, whatever the barrels of water that drench the sacrifice and the wood on which it lies, we shall be kept steadfast, unmovable, always abounding in the work of the Lord, gaining by our losses, succeeding by our failures, triumphing in our defeats, and ever more conquerors through Him who loves us.

17

Acts 20:22

GATHERING CLOUDS

I know Thee, who hast kept my path, and made
Light for me in the darkness, tempering sorrow
So that it reached me like a solemn joy.

Browning

*A*fter the great uproar excited by Demetrius was over, Paul sent for his disciples to come to his place of hiding and exhorted them. He commended them to the grace of God and took a sad farewell. This done, he departed to go into Macedonia by way of Troas (Acts 20:1).

For the story of the next few months, we must turn to Paul's second epistle to the Corinthians, the most remarkable of his epistles for its revelation of his heart. Bengel calls it an itinerary, and Dean Stanley says that the very stages of Paul's journey are impressed on it, while a third says that the strong emotions under which it was written make it more difficult to translate than any other.

At Troas, which he now visited for a second time, the apostle expected to meet Titus, who had probably been the bearer of the first epistle to Corinth—a letter elicited by the sad story of the dissensions and disorders of their church that had been brought to Ephesus by members of the household of Chloe. Paul had dealt with the whole situation in very stringent terms and was intensely anxious to learn the result of his words. Often since writing, Paul had questioned whether he might not have risked his entire influence for good over his converts and driven them into defiance and despair. The delay of Titus confirmed his worst fears, and though a great door of ministry was opened at Troas, he could find no relief for his perturbed and eager spirit, but taking leave of them, he went forth into Macedonia (2 Cor. 2:13).

In all probability, Paul headed immediately for the beloved Philippi. But even there, since no tidings of Titus were at hand, his flesh had no relief. He was afflicted on every side; without were fightings, and within were fears.

At last, God who comforts the lowly comforted Paul by the coming of the overdue traveler. Paul was glad not only to have his friend at his side but also to learn that the effect of his first letter had been wholesome and had led to an outbreak of godly repentance and affectionate yearning to himself. It was after conference with Titus on the whole state of affairs at Corinth that he wrote his second epistle.

HIS MULTIPLIED SORROWS

Throughout the second epistle to the Corinthians, Paul speaks of the great anguish through which he was passing. And while he refutes the many unkind and slanderous allegations made against him, he does so with powerful references to his sufferings.

The treasure, Paul says, was in an earthen vessel. He was pressed, perplexed, pursued, and smitten down, always bearing about in the body the dying of the Lord Jesus. Paul's outward man was decaying; many groans escaped him, being burdened, and he often longed to be absent from the body that he might be present with the Lord.

In one of the most extraordinary enumerations of antitheses in any language, he mentions, among other sources of anguish, his spells of sleeplessness, his repeated fastings, the blows, imprisonments, tumults, toils, and pressure of his daily life. But there must have been other and deeper reasons—perhaps that he was being so persistently maligned and his teachings so flagrantly misrepresented, or because the love of many was waxing cold, or that the infant churches, on which he had expended so many prayers and tears, were proving themselves unworthy. But however these things might be, the sufferings of Christ seem almost to have submerged him.

But the Father of mercies and God of all comfort drew near and comforted him. There were many notes in that sweet and tender refrain that stole on the heart of His afflicted servant. The testimony of Paul's conscience was that he had worked in sincerity and holiness—the divine faithfulness that never gave sign of fickleness or failure, the light of the knowledge of God that shone clear in his soul, the thanksgiving of many to God that arose through his sorrows, the vision of the eternal weight of glory, the earnest of the Spirit in his soul and the sure anticipation of the building of God that awaited him in the heavens, the blessed sense of being an ambassador of Christ and a fellow worker with God. God knows how to comfort, and fountains of divine consolation arose from unknown depths for him, as they will for you and me. And thus, though the outward man decay, the inward man will be renewed day by day.

But in spite of all, this deeply suffering soul never diminished for a moment its devoted labors for the cause of God. His letters abound with references to the offertory that he was raising for the poverty-stricken saints at Jerusalem from all the churches he had established. Now he stimulates Corinth by citing the example of Macedonia; and again he enumerates the precautions against the slanders of those who alleged that he was profiting by the contributions. There are indications also of his labors, not only toward the churches that knew and revered him but also in new and unexplored regions. Being ambitious to preach the gospel where Christ had not been already named and unwilling to build on another man's foundation, Paul fully preached the gospel even to Illyricum on the Adriatic.

Oh, incomparable man, no weights could hold back the flight of your devoted spirit! Nay, as the child's kite must be weighted to make it soar the higher, so did your sorrows give you new yearnings over souls, new ambitions for your Lord! You have your reward in the love of Gentile hearts, until the sundown of the present age, as you had your glorying in Christ Jesus in things pertaining to God. We magnify Christ in you, for we fully realize that He worked through you for the obedience of the Gentiles, by word and deed, in the power of signs and wonders, and in the power of the Holy Spirit (Rom. 15:18–19).

HIS FRIENDS

Some men have a marvelous power in attaching men to themselves. They possess a kind of spiritual magnetism for others, who gather to their heart and follow their lead. Paul had this power in a superlative degree. He was loved as few have been loved, and he loved in return. It must have therefore been a peculiar pleasure to him, as at last he came to Corinth, to find himself the center of a great assemblage of devoted friends.

There was Timothy, his "beloved child," his "true child in faith"; Tychicus, "a beloved brother and faithful minister in the Lord," who was with him in his last imprisonment; Titus, his "partner and fellow helper," his "own son after the common faith"; Luke, "the beloved physician," who accompanied him to Rome and was with him to the last; Trophimus, the Ephesian, who would have been with him to death had not sickness detained him at Miletus; Aristarchus and Secundus, the former of whom probably contrived to become his fellow prisoner that he might minister to his illustrious friend; Sosipater, his kinsman, well known to the Roman church; Gaius, a trophy of that first missionary tour that had taken him to Derbe; and the other Gaius, at this time his host; and Jason, who had sheltered him at Thessalonica at the risk of his life.

And these were only a handful of the great harvest of his friends. Writing at this time from Corinth, he greets twenty-six persons by name in the closing verses of the epistle to the Romans. Priscilla and Aquila, who had laid down their necks for him (v. 4); the beloved Epanetus; Amplias, his "beloved in the Lord"; Persis, the beloved; and many others. If he were more bitterly hated than most, he had a greater recompense of love than most, and his course through the world was constantly gathering around it the wealth of human hearts. And what love in the annals of Love is comparable to that which unites souls in Christ?

Hearts I have won of sister or of brother,

Quick on the earth or hidden in the sod,
Lo, every heart awaiteth me, another
Friend in the blameless family of God.

What blessed fellowship these elect souls must have had at Corinth during those memorable three months in which the epistles to the Galatians and the Romans were being written! Probably those masterly arguments were first given in their reverent and attentive hearing. To them was uttered the first rough draft of Romans 5 and 8 or of Galatians 3 and 5. The conversations—carried far on into the night—on the destiny of Israel, the counsels of God, the method of dealing with the uneasiness of weak consciences, may have engaged eager and intense discussion.

At last it became necessary for the party to break up. Paul was eager to get to Jerusalem for the Passover, and a passage had been taken for him in one of the pilgrim vessels that started each spring from every port on the Aegean for Palestine. Before his embarking, however, a plot was discovered on the part of the Jews for his assassination, and he was compelled to alter his route, going with an escort of friends through Macedonia and taking up a sailing vessel from Troas. He took advantage of this change in his plans to say another farewell to the endeared circle at Philippi, always nearest his heart, and then hastened to rejoin the little band that awaited him at Troas, sworn to care for him and the treasure that he had been at such pains to collect.

Sad Forebodings

That journey from Troas down the ragged shores of Asia Minor, sailing by day and anchoring by night, must in some senses have been sadder to the little band of devoted followers than to Paul.

Paul had no doubt as to its direction. He went bound in the spirit to Jerusalem, sure that there, as in every other city, bonds and afflictions awaited him. Of this the Holy Spirit gave unequivocal testimony. Paul prolonged his speech at Troas till midnight and sent for the elders of the Ephesian church to meet him at Miletus because he knew that all they among whom he had gone about preaching the Kingdom should see his face no more. He said farewell to the little groups, who waved their goodbyes across the waters to his receding ship, as though it were his last. What the Spirit said through the disciples at Tyre only corroborated what He had said to the heart of Paul (Acts 20:23). What Agabus foretold in striking symbolism had been prognosticated already by that inward prophet whose voice cannot be bribed. Though Paul was quite willing to adopt any course of action that James might suggest with the view of keeping him pent up in the upper platform of the temple and away from the streets filled at feast time with excited crowds, Paul knew it would not avail. It did not surprise Paul when he found himself the center of a frenzied mob, hurrying him down the temple steps to the lower court, where they meant to take his life without sacrilege to the holy shrine.

To those who loved him, the successive and unanimous prognostications of coming disaster were like the descent of a coffin containing the earthly remains of one's dearest friend. Luke gives us a moving picture of the scene in the house of Philip, their host at Caesarea, with whom Paul must have exchanged tender reminiscences of Stephen. Agabus came there from Jerusalem, and unbinding Paul's girdle bound himself with it, speaking in the power of the Holy Ghost and announcing that in like manner the Jews would bind its owner. "And," says Luke, "when we heard these things, both we, and they of that place, besought him not to go up to Jerusalem" (Acts 21:12). They wept hard enough, Paul said, to break his heart.

But he was marvelously sustained. It seemed as though he were going rather to a wedding than to a funeral. Was not his spirit espoused to his Lord, and would not death land him in His presence, which was far better than the choice society of his friends? He was ready not only to be bound but to die at Jerusalem for the name of the Lord Jesus. Indeed, he held not his life of any account, as dear unto himself, in comparison with accomplishing his course and the ministry that he had received of the Lord Jesus, to testify the gospel of the grace of God.

> Yea, thro' life, death, thro' sorrow and thro' sinning,
> He shall suffice me, for He hath sufficed;
> Christ is the end, for Christ was the beginning,
> Christ the beginning, for the end is Christ.

18

Philippians 1:12–13

THE FURTHERANCE OF THE GOSPEL

My soul exults to dwell secure,
Thy strong munitions round her;
She dares to count her triumphs sure,
Nor fears lest hell confound her;
Though tumults startle earth and sea,
Thou changeless Rock! they shake not Thee.

Ray Palmer

*T*he one thing Paul cared for most was "the furtherance of the gospel" (Phil. 1:12). If only the gospel of the love of God made progress and the Lord Jesus were magnified, Paul was more than content to suffer to the uttermost. And now, as he reviews the things that had happened to him from the standpoint of the years, he rejoices with exceeding joy to be able to announce to his brethren at Philippi that they had fallen out to the furtherance of the gospel.

Space forbids us to tell in detail the story of Paul's transportation from the lower platform of the temple at Jerusalem to the hired house at Rome. But we may at least consider its successive stages beneath the light of the thought that gave Paul such pleasure, that they had all opened the door to the furtherance of the gospel, partly

143

by giving him an opportunity of manifesting the traits of a true Christian character and partly by enabling him to give his testimony for Jesus before the highest tribunals in the world.

First, there was the awful riot in the temple court. The Jews of Asia, perhaps led by Alexander the coppersmith, laid hold of Paul, under the impression that he had introduced Trophimus, whom they knew as an Ephesian, into the court reserved for Jews. They dragged Paul down the steps, furiously beating him with the intent of murdering him when they reached the bottom. With the greatest difficulty, he was rescued by Lysias and his legionaries, who rushed down from the adjoining Castle of Antonia, surrounded him with their shields, and carried him back on their shoulders from the frenzied vehemence of the mob (Acts 21:31–36). It was not simply the result of natural coolness and self-command, but it was because Paul was at rest in Christ and desired to magnify his Master that he was able to hold a brief conversation with his Roman deliverer in the midst of the tumult and obtain permission to address the people in their national tongue, weaving the story of the risen Jesus so ingeniously into his personal narrative that they could do no other than listen.

There was a manly strength in Paul's quiet remonstrance with those who were set to examine him by scourging and in his declaration of Roman citizenship that must have filled them with profound respect. Here was no common criminal!

Some have questioned the propriety of his behavior, when on the following day he was arraigned before the Sanhedrin. But Annas, who sat to judge him, had really been deposed from the high priesthood (though, as a matter of fact, he still exercised that office). And as to raising the question of the resurrection, that, after all, was the one point at issue between him and the Jews (Acts 23:6). The Pharisees professed to believe in the resurrection, and yet they refused to admit that Jesus had risen. Paul, on the other hand, sought to establish not only that there would be a resurrection but also that there had been one.

That his efforts to use these difficult situations for the glory of his Master were appreciated and accepted was made abundantly clear by the vision of the Lord, who told Paul to be of good cheer and assured him that the witness that he had given from the steps of the castle and in the halls of the Sanhedrin should be repeated in

Rome herself, at the very heart of the empire, where all the Gentiles should hear (Acts 23:11).

There must have been something very noble and heroic in Paul's bearing, for his nephew, who was evidently in on the secrets of Paul's foes and must have passed as a narrow-minded Jew, would never have run the risk of being torn from limb to limb for divulging the secret plot of the zealots (Acts 23:16). These men had bound themselves by a solemn vow neither to eat nor drink till they had forever silenced the tongue that gave them more cause to fear than all the legions of Felix's escort.

His judicial trials. Paul was presently hurried by a strong body of soldiers in a forced march through the night to Antipatris, thirty-five miles distant, and twenty-five miles farther, on the following day, to Caesarea to undergo trial before Felix, the Roman governor of Judea. But as on repeated occasions when Paul stood before him, he seemed less concerned about himself and bent on snatching every opportunity of so public a position to explain the nature of "the Way" and to reason with his judge concerning the faith in Christ Jesus (Acts 24). Indeed, on one occasion he spoke so powerfully in the presence of Felix and the woman with whom he was living in adultery of righteousness, self-control, and judgment to come that Felix trembled as the prisoner compelled him to review a life of shameless infamy beneath the searchlight of an awakened conscience.

When Festus came in the room of Felix, who had been recalled in disgrace, the apostle within a few days so far impressed the newcomer with his faith in Jesus, who had died but whom he affirmed to be alive, that the governor was able to state the case with wonderful accuracy to King Agrippa, who, with his sister Bernice, came to pay their respects to the new representative of the emperor (Acts 25, 26).

But perhaps Paul's greatest opportunity—and one of which he availed himself to the full—was that in which he was able to preach the gospel to an assembly that comprised all the fashion, wealth, and distinction of the land (Acts 25:23). Festus was there in state, and the Herods, brother and sister, were seated on golden chairs. The officers of the garrison and the principal men of the city were there. How great a contrast between the splendid pomp of that occasion and the poor chained prisoner at the judgment seat! Yet, in truth, though bending under the weight of sixty years and many sorrows, Paul was the noblest and fairest decked of all the glittering throng. How grandly he preached Christ that day under the guise of making his defense! The story of the suffering and risen Lord, the fulfillment of the predictions of Moses and the prophets, the opening of eyes, the turning from darkness to light, the conditions of remitted sin and an inheritance among the saints—such topics were recited with all the passionate earnestness of which he was capable. The Roman thought him mad, and the Jewish prince needed all his courtly wit to turn aside the barbed dart of the prisoner's appeal (Acts 26).

CAESAREA

In one of the guard rooms of the old palace of the Caesars, for two whole years Paul was kept a prisoner but was permitted to see and receive help from his friends. How gladly must the saints in Caesarea and from other places have availed themselves of the privilege! It is an old tradition that during this period Luke wrote the third gospel in fellowship with his friend and under his direction. If this were so, what an unfailing source of interest it must have been for the two men to trace the course of all things accurately from the first, as they delivered them, which from the beginning were eye-witnesses and ministers of the Word.

In another way, that period of two years was very fruitful in the best sense. Paul's appreciation of the truth as it is in Jesus was greatly ripened and deepened. Contrast the epistles to the *Thessalonians, Corinthians, Romans,* and *Galatians* with those to the *Ephesians, Philippians,* and *Colossians,* and the advance is easily discernible. There is less polemics and defense of his motives and actions and more of the believer's vital union with his Lord, less doctrinal discussion of the work of Christ and more absorption in His Person, less of the old covenant, more of the new, of the King, and of the life in the heavenlies. Ah, those years spent within view of the dividing sea, restrained by the old castle walls and the chain that he shook so pathetically before Festus and his guests, notwithstanding that the indomitable spirit was stayed from its incessant labors and journeys, were turned to good account if only they enabled him to give the Church his priceless prison epistles!

At last this term of confinement came to an end. The Jewish

authorities had never ceased to urge that Paul should be handed over to their jurisdiction, a claim that in God's good providence the Roman governors steadfastly refused. They knew, and Paul knew, that to such a trial there would be only one end. But finally, when Festus showed signs of yielding, Paul claimed his right as a Roman citizen to have his case tried by the emperor himself, partly because it would remove the case from local prejudice, partly because he desired to secure for the Christian Church the same recognition as was awarded to the Jewish synagogue, and partly that he might fulfill his long-cherished purpose of proclaiming the gospel in Rome.

To that appeal nothing to the contrary could be alleged. Paul had appealed to Caesar, and to Caesar he must go. As soon as possible, he was placed under the care of a centurion for conveyance to the imperial city.

THEN CAME THE VOYAGE

At every stage of it, the apostle seems to have bent all his endeavors to use his opportunities, as far as possible, for the glory of his Lord. For Paul, to live was Christ. Paul reckoned always and everywhere that he was a debtor to all men and under obligation to repay to each some proportion of the momentous debt he owed for his redemption.

They set sail first in an ordinary sailing vessel, then from Myra in an Alexandrian corn ship, one of the great fleet perpetually engaged in provisioning Rome. Contrary to the advice of Paul, who even at this stage of the voyage must have been considered as a person of distinction and experience, the captain attempted to cross the open bay from the Fair Havens to Phonice, each on the southern side of Crete. But when they were halfway across, the wind changed, and a sudden squall struck down from the mountains and carried the big ship out to sea (Acts 27:4-15). In the brief respite afforded of sailing under the lee of the little island of Clauda, they hauled in the boat that had been tearing through the water behind them and got ropes round the straining vessel to strengthen her. This done, there was nothing for it but to drift through the open sea. Three days later, all hands (even of the prisoners) were called in to lighten the ship by casting out cargo and other movables, and after many days of storm, in which neither sun nor moon appeared, all hope that they should be saved gradually faded away.

It was then that Paul stood forth, calm and assured, with the message of God to cheer and reanimate their fainting hearts. Like Peter before his execution, the servant of God had quietly slept amid the tumult. Like Peter, too, he had been ministered to by angels. Through the murky atmosphere, one of these ministering spirits had found his way to Paul's side, uttering a "Fear not!" fresh from the throne and an assurance that he should yet stand before Caesar (Acts 27:24). Evidently, the deliverance of the crew had been previously the subject of the apostle's prayer, for the angel added, "Lo, God hath given thee all them that sail with thee." Here was an opportunity of preaching faith in God and belief in the power of prayer.

Always full of prompt common sense, Paul detected the attempt of the sailors, when the vessel struck, to get away in the boat. But with something above common sense, with a sense of the eternal and divine, Paul took bread, and as though he were presiding at the Lord's table in Corinth or Philippi, he gave thanks to God in the presence of all, broke it, and began to eat.

When they reached the shore of Malta on that drear November morning, it seemed as though nothing more could be done to further the gospel. But as the viper fell off Paul's hand, and the father of the chief man in the island was healed of dysentery through his prayer, and everyone else who had diseases throughout the island were cured by his touch, much was done to magnify Christ, concerning whom Paul was proud to say, "Whose I am, and whom I serve" (Acts 27:23).

So To Rome

Did Paul's heart trouble him as he at last approached the city and signs of her splendor and teeming life multiplied at every step? Paul had often thought of this moment and longed for it. Some three years before, writing to the church at Rome, he said, "I long to see you, that I may impart unto you some spiritual gift" (Rom. 1:11). He confessed that he had often prayed and purposed to come to them. But he had never anticipated coming like this—one of a knot of prisoners in charge of Roman legionaries. But almost certainly through his bonds, Paul was able to effect very much more good than if he had been free. Had he been free, he might have gone from synagogue to synagogue, but the opportunity would never have befallen him of speaking to the Praetorian guard and Caesar's household.

It is thus that God answers our prayers in ways and methods we did not expect. We have set our hearts on realizing some project. For long years it has gleamed before us as an Alp through its long-drawn valley. We have yearned, prayed, and worked for it night and day. Assurances have been borne in upon our souls that one day we shall rejoice in a realization of our cherished desires. But when at last we come to our Rome, it is as prisoners and our hands in fetters.

God fulfilled Paul's desire to see Rome in this way probably for two reasons. First, for safety's sake, and second, for the wider audience that awaited him. And these two reasons may necessitate our being conducted to our Rome in chains. Were it otherwise, the very exuberance of our joy might intoxicate or the gratification of our ambition might overbalance. It is best to have the chain. Not Rome without the chain, nor the chain without Rome, but Rome and the chain together.

Do not fret at the limitations and disabilities of your life. They are required as the balance to your life and constitute your opportunity. Storm and shipwreck, centurion and sea captain, soldier and fetter, Caesarea and Rome—all are part of the plan, all work together for good, all are achieving God's ideal and making you what, in your best hours, you have asked to become.

19

MORE ABUNDANTLY
THAN THEY ALL

Would I describe a preacher, such as Paul,
Were he on earth, would hear, approve, and own—
Paul should himself direct me.

Cowper

"God," says the eloquent Adolphe Monod, "left to the Jews the first twelve apostles, and gave to the Gentiles one only, whom He prepared expressly for them. Like a spiritual Atlas, Paul carries the whole heathen world upon his shoulders. That Roman empire, the most powerful on the face of the earth, which required seven ages to be established, he took only a quarter of an age to regenerate. The greatest among men was Jesus Christ; the greatest among apostles was Paul."

Even in these days of easy and universal communication, the apostle's record as a traveler would have been a remarkable one. But how much more remarkable it appears when we recall the bandits that infested the mountain passes of Asia Minor, the impetuous torrents that crossed the track, the vast distances that had to be traversed on foot, the hardships of the wayside inns and caravansaries, and the suspicion and dislike of which Jews must have always been the object.

But what a record Paul has left! In his *first* missionary journey, he establishes churches as Christian garrisons along the central highway of Asia Minor and attracts the enthusiastic Gauls with the tenderest affection—"preaching both to Jews and Gentiles, converting a proconsul and silencing a false prophet; at one time adored as a god, at another stoned by the same people in their fury." In his *second*, Paul proclaims the gospel to Europe and founds churches in some of the most famous and influential cities—Philippi, Thessalonica, Berea, Athens, and Corinth flame out as successive beacon fires in the darkness. In the *third*, like a Colossus, Paul strides the Aegean, planting one foot in Asia Minor and the other in Greece, where he preaches even to Illyricum. In the *fourth*, after pleading his cause before at least three different tribunals, Paul traverses the Mediterranean, saves the crew and passengers of the storm-driven corn ship by his prayers and heroism, compels the respect and affection of an island of barbarians, and reaches Rome in the guise of a prisoner, but really as a conqueror, to unfurl the banner of his Master in the palace of the Caesars. *After his release,* Paul again sets forth on journeys that carry him perhaps to Spain but certainly to familiar scenes in Asia Minor and Greece. So he fulfills his course till Rome and martyrdom again come in sight.

When Paul began his work, the world was being borne to its grave in spite of what philosophy, literature, and legislation could do to arrest its moral decay. But when Paul closed his work, some thirty years afterward, seeds of life and salvation had been sown and even nurtured into sturdy growth that were destined, after three centuries, to displace the decaying remnants of heathenism with the fresh young undergrowth of Christian civilization.

We may well inquire into the secret of this marvelous work to which, after that of our Lord, the position of Christianity in the world at this moment is to be ascribed. And if we do, we shall discover it not in his intellectual talent and eloquent speech, for these were more than neutralized by his physical weaknesses (2 Cor. 10:10), his "thorn" (12:7), and his "contemptible" utterance (10:10). But Paul's secret was in sources of power that are within the reach of us all, however greatly we may come short of the commanding equipment that, in the words of the great leader, would have made him, had he sought it, shine in the highest rank among the wise and the orators of all ages, so that he would not have been second to any of those masters of thought or of language of whom ancient Greece boasted.

In the forefront, we must place the apostle's vivid remembrance of the mercy that had been shown him. "I obtained mercy," he says on one occasion (1 Tim. 1:13), when attempting to explain the sources of his indomitable perseverance through shameful condemnation, smiting down, and daily dying. It was as though he never could forget how deeply he had sinned and how strenuously he had resisted the very grace that he now proclaimed. Paul was constantly returning to this precious thought. How could he ever despair of men, since such a one as he had found mercy? How could he faint, when the same grace that had laid hold of him waited to enable him? How could he ever repay the long-suffering that had brooded over his storm-driven nature and had abounded over his rebellion until it made him a trophy of its power? Like a silver refrain, it came back on him in all times of anguish, distress, and virulent opposition: I obtained mercy, therefore I dare not, must not faint (2 Cor. 4:1).

From the commencement to the close of his career, Paul was impelled by the one master thought that he had been redeemed to serve, saved that he might save others. The memory of what he had been saved from and saved to was the constant incentive of his arduous and exhausting toils. And so it is well for us, if we can get away for a time from the bustle and rush of life, to stand beneath the cross where Jesus died, realizing that every drop from His every wound appeals to our every heartbeat to spend or be spent for the cause that cost Him so dear.

Closely connected with this, we must mention the great and simple purpose for which the apostle lived. He bent his strength to save men, and for this he was prepared to make any sacrifice. He was equally careful to the very last to institute and organize the little Christian communities that were absolutely necessary to conserve and develop the spiritual life that had been implanted. But all such purposes were subordinated to that "which trieth our hearts" (1 Thess. 2:4). It mattered comparatively little what were the outward results of his endeavors or what men might say or do, so long as he had the testimony shed through his heart that it pleased God.

This motive is viewed under another light when, in the next

epistle, he yearns that "the name of our Lord Jesus Christ may be glorified" (2 Thess. 1:12). We cannot forget that the passion of Christ's heart during His earthly ministry was to glorify His Father, and there was a similar passion in the heart of Paul to glorify the Son. To the end of Paul's ministry, that purpose grew even stronger. It was always his earnest expectation and hope that in nothing he should be ashamed, but that as always, so then, Christ should be magnified in his body, whether by life or death (Phil. 1:20).

Would that this also were our single aim! It would greatly simplify our lives. We are apt to set ourselves on the accomplishment of purposes that, though good in themselves, come short of the best. And when we do not succeed in them, when the revival does not ensue or hosts of souls are not converted or the Church does not heed, we are apt to write hard things against ourselves and God. Whereas, if we simply sought the good pleasure and glory of our Master, we should discover that we succeed amid apparent failure and are more than conquerors when fleeing for our lives.

Happy is the man who can appeal from the verdict of obvious results, of his fellows, of the inner circle of dearest friends, and even of his own heart, and say, "But with me it is a very small thing that I should be judged of you, or of man's judgment: yea, I judge not mine own self. For I know nothing by myself; yet am I not hereby justified: but he that judgeth me is the Lord. Therefore judge nothing before the time, until the Lord come, who both will bring to light the hidden things of darkness, and will make manifest the counsels of the hearts: and then shall every man have praise of God" (1 Cor. 4:3-5).

To each of us is committed a stewardship of wealth or time or influence or talent in thought and speech. With Paul, each of us can say, "A dispensation of the gospel is committed unto me" (1 Cor. 9:17). Now surely it is required in stewards not that they should realize all the dreams that suggest themselves to their imagination but that they be found faithful to Him who appointed them. Judge your lives not by results but by your motives and by the smile of His good pleasure who appointed you.

His plan of living also greatly ministered to his success. In point of fact, Paul had no plan at all. For him, the way had been prepared in the counsels of God before the worlds were made, and he had only to discover its track. The scheme of the temple of his life had been conceived by the divine Architect. Paul had only to get it by communion with Him on the Mount. He need do nothing from himself, in the sense of self-origination, but do what he saw his Savior doing. Paul's one aim was to repeat in the time sphere what *He* was doing in the unseen and eternal.

This made the apostle so cautious in referring to his future program. Whatever should happen, he must keep in the current of the will of God. To "purpose according to the flesh, that with me there should be the yea yea, and nay nay" of human forecast was foreign to the habit of his mind (2 Cor. 1:17). He was ever living in such dependence on the Holy Spirit for guidance and for the unfolding of the divine purpose that from some apparently trivial circumstance he would "gather" the movements of the pillar of cloud by day and of fire by night. And there was no interval between his apprehension of the divine purpose and his endeavor to take up his tent and follow wherever it might lead (Acts 16:6–7).

When in the present century the purpose presented itself of completing that magnificent specimen of Gothic architecture, the Cologne Cathedral, it was not necessary to prepare a plan for gathering up and carrying forward the results of previous centuries into a symmetrical and beautiful edifice. The architect to whom the task of completion was entrusted had but to bring out and study the plan as it was first conceived by Meister Gerard in the thirteenth century and as it is still preserved in his own pen-and-ink outlines. So Christian workers should never forget the injunctions—four times repeated of Moses—of making all things according to the pattern shown them on the Mount. The pattern of the Body of Christ, of the position of each individual believer among its members, and of the work that each should accomplish was fixed before the worlds were made. "What did You mean for me, O God, in my creation, redemption, and the ordering of my life? Teach me to do Your will, for You are my God. Your Spirit is good: lead me into the land of uprightness." Such should be the prayer of each Christian worker.

But, perhaps, the secret of Paul's success lay most of all in his faculty of extracting power from his weaknesses. He had eminent gifts of character, of energy, of power to command and lead and organize, of thought and speech. But had it not been for the presence of Paul's infirmity, he might never have become the great apostle of the Gentiles or accomplished such splendid work. He might have yielded to self-confidence in his heart depths and relied on these extraordinary endowments instead of casting himself absolutely, as he was compelled to do, on the power of God. His lifework was accomplished not by himself but by God operating through the frail organism of his mortal body.

Judging from the words of his detractors which he seems to endorse, his bodily presence was weak and his speech contemptible (2 Cor. 10:10), the former phrase referring to his thorn in the flesh, of which we have spoken, and the latter to a lack of those graces of oratory that the Greeks were accustomed to expect from their public teachers. It was very humbling to the flesh, but it drained away the last remains of human pride and left Paul, as the forty years in the desert left Moses, a vessel prepared for the Master's use because so utterly dependent on the Master's hand to direct and empower.

In his early life, Paul was one of Gamaliel's most promising pupils—strong, self-reliant, vehement, clear in thought, incisive in speech, swift in action. Among the men of his age, few could outmatch Saul of Tarsus, who earlier than was customary became a member of the Jewish Sanhedrin. Would you recognize Paul in the weakness, the fear, and the much trembling of this broken man? Or if you did, might you not be tempted to regret that he had opposed Christ in his strength and had brought only weakness into his service? But such request would be wholly unnecessary. Had Paul been strong, he might have been—we borrow the expression—an Apollos, a Chrysostom, an Augustine, a Luther, but never Paul. Because he was weak, he was strong; because he bore chains, he was the great emancipator from chains; because he was poor, he succeeded in making so many rich.

After this, let no one complain. The only thing of which we need to be sure is whether we have been called of God to certain work for Him. Then, if limitations and hindrances suggest the impossibility of ever accomplishing it, let us dare to glory in them and discover in their presence the ground for believing that we have been selected for the work to which they might threaten to become a fatal barrier. In other words, let us do by faith the work that others do by human might.

Another element in the success of the apostle's work must be found in his denial of self. He had large and expansive views of truth and life and could probably have permitted to himself many things that he carefully refrained from lest his influence for Christ should be impaired. In 1 Corinthians 8:13, Paul tells us that if meat should make his brother to offend, he will eat no flesh while the world last. In 1 Corinthians 8:7–9, he explains that though as far as his own conscience was concerned, he could eat in an idol's temple without condemnation, yet he dare not do it lest he should cast a stumblingblock before the undecided, halting feet of some weak disciple. In 1 Corinthians 9 he alleges his determination to forego the delights of wife and child though his was a very tender nature, to forego the support that his converts might voluntarily offer though he had as much right to take it as the oxen did their corn or priests their share of temple offerings. And at the close of that chapter, Paul explains how carefully he kept his body under, bringing it into subjection lest he should fail to do the utmost possible for the souls of men and compel the Lord to substitute an instrument more suited for His purpose. In 2 Corinthians 6:3, Paul speaks of giving no offense in anything, that the ministry might not be blamed.

This, too, is a path in which we may follow the steps of this great servant of Jesus. All Christian workers, zealous for the coming of God's Kingdom, must at once forego indulgences and practices that are not in themselves unlawful, that the ministry may not be blamed or souls hindered. Consideration of the effect that may be produced upon others is a very real and urgent factor in determining our action with regard to matters that lie in the great twilight borderland between what is clearly defined as right and clearly defined as wrong. The more widespread our influence over others, the more absolute the necessity of considering the effect on others of methods and actions in which we are left with large liberty of self-determination and choice.

In this enumeration, let us not forget the eloquence of his tears. "Remember," he said to the elders of the Ephesian church, "that by the space of three years I ceased not to warn every one night and day with tears" (Acts 20:31). Every word is significant! Not content with appealing to them by day, he is compelled to push on into the nights when, worn by emotion, labor, and teaching, his tired body might surely claim its rest. Nor was this an occasional burst of devotion to be followed by spells of indolence and lethargy. He did not cease this ministry for three long years but pursued it without relaxation, without interruption, without pause. Nor was this work carried out with the persistence of a zealot or the eagerness of a partisan but was pursued with the tears of a soul lover.

"Do not complain," says the eloquent writer already quoted, "of his importunity! You, unthankful, he disturbs but once; his own repose is broken every night, if not for you, for others. Nay, more; whatever you are, he will not let you go until he has obtained— what? Some favor, some kindness? Ah! the greatest favor, the greatest kindness you can manifest is to be converted to the Lord Jesus Christ, or to serve him with greater fidelity. You refuse him, you repulse him, notwithstanding his entreaties; but before you leave him, look at him—he weeps. He weeps over the sins in which you continue; over the injury your example does to the Church; over the stumbling-block you set before the world; and, above all, for the future you are preparing for yourself. What do you say to this apostle in tears before you—I was going to say prostrate at your feet? The God whom he serves once summed up in a single sentence all that his apostle ought to be: 'Behold, he prayeth.' You—now in your turn, you to whom he preaches, may sum up all that he does for you in a single sentence—behold, he weeps."

Why is it that Paul's fount of tears seems denied us? We have tears for many other things than the infinite loss of those who have rejected the gospel. For this, alas! no single drop trickles along the dry water channels. We are smitten by a terrible drought, our heart a very Sahara. Our water springs are frozen by remorseless cold or scorched by relentless heat. In losing the power of tears, we have lost one great power of causing them. It is by broken hearts that hearts are broken, by wet eyes that eyes are made to brim over with the waters of repentant sorrow.

Lastly, let us not forget the apostle's individual interest in his converts. "Warning *every one of you* night and day with tears" is one evidence of this, and for another we turn instinctively to Colossians 1:28: "Whom we preach, warning *every man,* and teaching *every man* in all wisdom; that we may present *every man* perfect in Christ Jesus." How he dwells on that phrase, "every man"! Paul had no sympathy with the reckless haste that shakes the boughs of the fruit trees to obtain their precious harvest. He knew too well the peril of injuring the delicate bloom. All the fruit he gathered for God was handpicked. Paul was more fond of the hand net than the seine. Like his Master, he would go far out of his way if he might cast the demon out of one possessed spirit or persuade an Agrippa to become a Christian. One soul, for whom Christ died, was in Paul's sight of unspeakable worth.

But underlying all these, there was the fundamental belief that it was not he but the grace of God that was with him and the power of God that worked through him. Paul energized according to the energy of One mightier than himself, who energized in him mightily. He worked, yet not he, but Christ worked in him. Anything save what Christ worked in him was wood, hay, and stubble, of which he dared not take account. He did not work for Christ but offered himself to Him without reserve, that Christ might penetrate and irradiate the inmost recesses of his being and then, through its cleansed panes, go forth to illuminate the hearts of men. All his care was to purify himself, that he might at all times be ready for the Master's use. His one desire was to yield himself to God and that his members might be used as weapons in the great conflict against the powers of hell.

This is, after all, the first and last lesson for the Christian worker: be clean, pure of heart, and simple in motive. See to it that there is no friction between your will and Christ's. Subdue your own activities as much as your own natural lethargy. Stand still till God impels you. Wait till He works in you to will and to do of His good pleasure. Exercise faith that God should accomplish in you the greatest results possible to the capacity of your nature. Let there be no thought of what you can do for God but all thought of what God can do through you. Nothing will make you so intense and ceaseless in your activity as this.

There will be an end of cowardice and of pride. Cowardice will cease because you will find yourself borne along by an irresistible impulse. Pride will end because you will have no occasion to boast. As soon might Milton's pen have been proud of writing *Paradise Lost* as you of what Christ may have done through you. "Shall the axe boast itself against him that heweth therewith? or shall the saw magnify itself against him that shaketh it?" (Isa. 10:15).

These words apply to us all, not less to those whom God has given the ministry of suffering and pain, the care of little children, the daily round of familiar duty. In these we minister to Him who judges, not by the character but by the spirit of our work, not by its extent but by its depth, not by results but by the spirit that animates and inspires.

In all such there is the certainty of the gracious cooperation of the Holy Spirit. Whenever they stand up to speak, the Spirit of God bears witness to their words so that they come with His demonstration to prepared hearts. Wherever they bear witness, whether by lip or life, the results that accrue testify to the presence and power of One mightier than they. And whenever they cross the threshold of some new soul or home or land, men become aware that the gospel has come to them, not in word only but also in power and in the Holy Ghost and in much assurance. Be it ours so to live, testify, and minister, that we may be workers not needing to be ashamed, good stewards of God's manifold grace, co-workers with God, ambassadors through whom God Himself may beseech men to be reconciled.

20

Philippians 1:23

TO BE
WITH CHRIST

With the patriarch's joy
They call I follow to the Land unknown;
I trust in Thee, and know in whom I trust;
Or life or death is equal—neither weighs!
All weight in this—oh, let me live to Thee!

Young

*T*hrough the providence of God, and probably by the kind intervention of the centurion—who had developed a sincere admiration for Paul during their months of travel together and who, indeed, owed him his life—Paul, on his arrival in Rome, was treated with great leniency. He was permitted to hire a house or apartment in the near neighborhood of the great Praetorian barracks and live by himself, the only sign of his captivity consisting in the chain that fastened his wrist to a Roman legionary—the soldiers relieving each other every four or six hours.

There were many advantages in this arrangement. It secured Paul from the hatred of the Jewish people and gave him a marvelous opportunity of casting the seeds of the gospel into the head of the rivers of population that poured from the metropolis throughout the known world. At the same time, it must have been very irksome. Always to be in the presence of another, and that other filled with Gentile antipathy to Jewish habits and pagan irresponsiveness to Christian fervor; to be able to make no movement without the clanking of his chain and the consent of his custodian; to have to conduct his conferences, utter his prayers, and write his epistles beneath those stolid eyes or amid brutal and blasphemous inter-ruptions—all this must have been excessively trying to a sensitive temperament like the apostle's. It must have been the hard and long schooling that had taught him to be content even with this, for the sake of the gospel. But this, also, he could do through Christ who strengthened him. And it also turned out greatly to the furtherance of the cause he loved. Many of these brawny veterans became hum-ble, earnest disciples. With a glow of holy joy, he informs the Philippians that his bonds in Christ have become manifest through-out the whole Praetorian guard. And we know that this was the beginning of a movement destined within three centuries to spread throughout the entire army, compelling Constantine to adopt Christianity as the religion of the State. This was a blessed issue of that period of suffering that so often extorted the cry, "Remember my bonds" (Col. 4:18).

Three days after his arrival in Rome, Paul summoned to his tem-porary lodging the leaders of the Jewish synagogues. There were said to have been synagogues for the sixty thousand Jews who were the objects of the dislike and ridicule of the imperial city. At the first interview, they cautiously occupied neutral ground and expressed the wish to hear and judge for themselves concerning the sect that was known to them only as the butt of universal condemnation. At the second interview, after listening to Paul's explanations and appeals for an entire day, there was the usual division of opinion. "Some believed the things which were spoken, and some believed not" (Acts 28:24). Paul's testimony having thus been first offered according to his invariable practice to his own people, there was now no further obstacle to his addressing a wider audience. The message of salvation was sent to the Gentiles, who would certainly hear (Acts 28:28). We are not, therefore, surprised to be told that for the next two years while his accusers were preparing their case or the emperor was permitting shameless indulgence to interfere with the discharge of public business, "[He] received all that came in unto him, preaching the kingdom of God, and teaching those things which concern the Lord Jesus Christ, with all confidence, no man forbidding him" (Acts 28:30–31).

It might be said of the apostle, as of his Lord, that they came to him from every quarter. Timothy, his son in the faith (1 Tim. 1:2); Mark now "profitable for the ministry" (2 Tim. 4:11); Luke, with his quick physician's eye and delicate sympathy; Aristarchus, who shared his imprisonment with Paul (Col. 4:10); Tychicus, from Ephesus, "beloved brother and faithful minister in the Lord" (Eph. 6:21); Epaphras, from Colossae, a beloved fellowservant and faithful minister of Christ (Col. 1:7), on the behalf of the church there; Epaphroditus, from Philippi, who brought the liberal contributions of the beloved circle that for so many years had never ceased to remember their friend and teacher (Phil. 4:18); Demas, who had not yet allowed the present to turn him aside from the eternal and unseen (2 Tim. 4:10)—these and others are mentioned in the postscripts of Paul's epistles as being with him. Members of the Roman church would always be welcomed and must have poured into his humble lodging in a perpetual stream: Epaenetus and Mary, Andronicus and Junia, Tryphena and Tryphosa, Persis the beloved, and Apelles the approved must often have gone to that apartment, which was irradiated with the perpetual presence of the Lord. They had come to meet him on his first arrival as far as the Appii Forum and the Three Taverns and would not be likely to neglect him now that he was settled among them.

Then what interest would be aroused by the episodes of those two years! The illness of Epaphroditus, who was sick unto death; the discovery and conversion of Onesimus, the runaway slave; the writing and dispatch of the epistles that bear such evident traces of the prison cell. There could have been no lack of incident amid the interest of which the two years must have sped by more swiftly than the other two years spent in confinement at Caesarea.

It is almost certain that Paul was acquitted at his first trial and liberated, then permitted for two or three years at least to engage again in his beloved work. He was evidently expecting this when, writing to the Philippians, he said: "But I trust in the Lord that I also myself shall come shortly" (2:24). In his letter to Philemon, he goes so far as to ask that a lodging may be prepared for him, as he hopes to be granted to their prayers (v. 22). Universal tradition affirms an interspace of liberty between his two imprisonments, and without this hypothesis, it is almost impossible to explain many of the incidental allusions of the epistles to Timothy and Titus that cannot refer, so far as we can see, to the period that falls within the compass of the Acts.

Whether Paul's liberation was due to the renewed efforts of the centurion or to more explicit reports received from Caesarea, history does not record. But it was by the decree of One greater than Nero that the coupling chain was struck off the apostle's wrist and he was free to go where he would. That he should abide in the flesh was, in the eye of the great Head of the Church, needful for the furtherance and joy of faith to the little communities that looked to him as their father. Their rejoicing was destined to be more abundant in Jesus Christ by Paul's coming to them again (Phil. 1:25–26).

Once more a free man, Paul would certainly fulfill his intention of visiting Philemon and the church of Colossae. Then he would make his way to the church at Ephesus to hold further discussion with them on those sacred mysteries that in his epistle he had commenced to unfold. It was probably during his residence there that Onesiphorus ministered to him with such tender thoughtfulness as to elicit a significant reference in the last epistle (2 Tim. 1:18). Leaving Timothy behind him with the injunction to command some that they should preach no other gospel than they had heard from his lips (1 Tim. 1:3), Paul traveled onward to Macedonia and Philippi. What a greeting must have been accorded to him there! They were his brethren, beloved and longed for, his joy and crown, whom he ever held in his heart and who in the defense and confirmation of the gospel had so deeply partaken with him. Lydia and Clement, Euodia and Syntyche, Epaphroditus and the jailer, together with many other fellow workers whose names are in the Book of Life, must have gathered around to minister to that frail, worn body to be inspired by that heroic soul.

From Philippi, Paul must have passed to other churches in Greece and among the rest to Corinth. Finally he set sail with Titus for Crete, where he left him to set in order the things that were needed and to appoint elders in every city (Tit. 1:5). On his return to the mainland, Paul wrote to Titus an epistle, from the closing messages in which we gather that he was about to winter at Nicopolis surrounded by several friends, such as Artemas, Zenas,

Tychicus, and Apollos, who were inspired with his own spirit and were gladly assisting him in strengthening the organization and purifying the teaching in these young churches. Each church seems to have passed through some such phases of doctrinal and practical difficulty as are reflected in the mirror of the epistles to Corinth (1 Cor. 3:12, 13).

This blessed liberty, however, was summarily cut short. One of the most terrible events in the history of the ancient world—the burning of Rome—took place in the year A.D. 64. To divert from himself the suspicion that indicated him as its author, Nero accused the Christians of being the incendiaries. Immediately, the fierce flames of the first general persecution broke out. Those who were resident in the metropolis and who must have been well known and dear to the apostle were seized and subjected to horrible barbarities while a strict search was made throughout the empire for their leaders—the Jews supporting the inquisitors. It was not likely that so eminent a Christian as the apostle would escape. The storm that sweeps the forest will smite first and most destructively the loftiest trees.

Paul was staying for a time at Troas, in the house of Carpus where he had arrived from Nicopolis. His arrest was so sudden that he had no time to gather up his precious books and parchments, which may have included copies of his epistles, a Hebrew Bible, and some early copies of the sayings of our Lord. It seems that he also left behind the cloak that had been his companion in many a wintry storm (2 Tim. 4:13). Then he was hurried to Rome.

A little group of friends accompanied him with faithful tenacity in this last sad journey. Demas and Crescens, Titus and Tychicus, Luke and Erastus. But Erastus remained at Corinth, through which the little band may have passed. Trophimus fell ill at Miletus and had to be left there, as the Roman guard would allow no delay. So for the second time, Paul reached Rome.

But the circumstances of his second imprisonment differed widely from those of the first. Then he had his own hired house; now he was left in close confinement, and tradition points to the Mamertine prison as the scene of his last weeks or months. Then he was easily accessible; now Onesiphorus had to seek him out very diligently, and it took some courage not to be ashamed of his imprisonment. Then he was the center of a large circle of friends and sympathizers; now the winnowing fan of trouble had greatly thinned their ranks, while others had been dispatched on distant missions. "Only Luke is with me" is the rather sad expression of the old man's loneliness (2 Tim. 4:11). Then he cherished a bright hope of speedy liberation; now, though he had successfully met the first impeachment, which was probably one of incendiarism, he had no hope of meeting the second, which would include the general charge of introducing new customs hostile to the stability of the imperial government. Its very vagueness made it so hard to combat, and it was inevitable that he should be caught within its meshes.

He was already being poured out as a libation, and the time had come for his loosing the anchor and setting sail. But it caused him no sorrow. In earlier days, he had greatly set his heart on being clothed upon with the body that was from heaven and on being suddenly caught up to be forever with the Lord. It seemed unlikely now that such would be the method of his transition to that rest of which he had spoken so movingly. Not by the triumphant path of the air but by the darksome path of death and the grave would he pass into the presence of the Lord. It was, however, a matter of small importance what would be the method of his homegoing. Paul was only too thankful on his review of his career to say humbly and truthfully, "I have fought a good fight, I have finished my course, I have kept the faith: henceforth there is laid up for me a crown of righteousness" (2 Tim. 4:7–8).

How characteristic it is to find him boasting of the great audience of Gentiles to whom, at the first stage of his trial, he was able fully to proclaim the gospel message. It is equally characteristic to hear him affirm that the ease and success of his witness bearing were due not to himself but to the conscious nearness of his Lord, who stood by and strengthened him.

What were the following processes of that trial? How long was he kept in suspense? Did Timothy arrive in time to see him and to be with him at the last supreme moment? What was the exact method of his martyrdom? To these questions there is no certain reply. Tradition points to a spot on the Ostian road, about three miles from Rome where, at the stroke of the headsman's axe, Paul was beheaded and, his spirit leaving its frail tenement, entered the house not made with hands, eternal in the heavens.

But how vast the contrast between that scene, which may have excited but little interest except to the friends who mingled in the little group, and that other scene, in which an abundant entrance was ministered to this noble spirit as it entered the presence of the Lord! If Christ arose to receive Stephen, may He not also have stood up to welcome Paul? Again Paul beheld the face that had looked down on him from the opened heavens at his conversion and heard the voice that had called him by his name. His long-cherished wish of being "with Christ" was gratified, and he found it "far better" than he had ever thought (Phil. 1:23).

His was now the inheritance of the saints in light, of which the Holy Spirit had been the down payment and firstfruits. He had passed the goal and attained to the prize of his high calling in Christ. He had been found in Christ, not having his own righteousness but having the righteousness that is of God by faith. No castaway was he! As he had kept Christ's deposit, so Christ had kept his. And as he gave in the account of his stewardship, who can doubt that the Lord greeted him with, "Well done, good and faithful servant; enter thou into the joy of thy Lord" (Matt. 25:23).

What a festal welcome Paul must have received from thousands whom he had turned from darkness to light, from the power of Satan unto God, and who were now to become his crown of rejoicing in the presence of the Lord! These from the highlands of Galatia, and those from the seaboard of Asia Minor. These from Judaistic prejudice, and those from the depths of Gentile depravity and sin. These from the degraded slave populations, and those from the ranks of the affluent and educated. Nor have such greetings ceased, but through all the centuries that have succeeded, there are comparatively few who have passed along "the Way to the Celestial City" who have not had to acknowledge a deep debt of gratitude to him who, of all others, was enabled to give a clearer apprehension of the divine method of justifying and saving sinners.

What share the blessed ones within the veil may have in the hastening of the second coming we cannot tell. But, surely, among those who eagerly anticipate that hour when the Bridegroom shall present the Church to Himself, without spot or wrinkle or any such thing, there is none more eager than he, who looked so constantly, even to the end, for the blessed hope, the appearance of the glorious Savior, and who did so much to prepare the Church for her Lord! And among the stones of the foundations of the New Jerusalem on which are written the names of the twelve apostles of the Lamb will surely be found at last that of Paul, who was before a blasphemer, a persecutor, and injurious but who obtained mercy and was counted faithful.

21

Galatians 6:11

How Large Letters

All his glowing language issued forth
With God's deep stamp upon its current worth.

Cowper

*I*t has been supposed, with much show of reason, that at the close of the epistle to the Galatians the apostle took the pen from the hand of his amanuensis and wrote somewhat more than his usual brief autograph. Generally, he contented himself with such words as those with which the epistle to the Colossians closes: "The salutation by the hand of me Paul. Remember my bonds. Grace be with you." But in the case of the Galatians, among whom his authority had been greatly impugned, it seemed incumbent to give rather more emphasis and importance to his words by a prolonged personal closing paragraph. He practically begs them excuse the clumsy shape and appearance of his handwriting on account of his defective sight, to which he may also be alluding when he touchingly describes himself as branded with the marks of Jesus (Gal. 6:17).

We may take his words also in a metaphorical sense. How largely his letters bulk in the makeup of the New Testament! If we judge the question only by comparing their length with that of the New Testament, we shall find that they make a fourth part of the whole. And their importance must be measured not by length but by weight. Before you put them into the scale, consider the precious treasures you are handling: the sublime chapter on love, 1 Corinthians 13; the matchless argument on justification in Romans 4—5; the glorious exposition of the work of the Holy Spirit in Romans 8; the triumphant resurrection hope of 1 Corinthians 15; the tender unveiling of the love between Jesus and His own in Ephesians. What priceless treasures are these that the Church owes first to the Holy Ghost and next to the apostle Paul, acting as His instrument! How many of the most precious and helpful passages in Scripture bear the mark of the tender, eager, fervent, and devout spirit of the apostle of the Gentiles!

The epistles marvelously reflect Paul's personality. It has been said of one of the great painters that he was accustomed to mixing his colors with blood drawn from a secret wound, and of Paul it may be said that he dipped his pen in the blood of his heart. Whatever impression had last rested on his sensitive nature colored the flow of his thoughts and expressions, whether it was the Philippian love expressed by the coming of Epaphroditus or the story of the Corinthian division told by the members of the house of Chloe. Probably it is for this very reason—because he wrote with all the freshness of speech, with the sparkle of conversation, as though he were talking naturally in a circle of friends—that he has so moved the heart of the world.

But it is not too much to say that humanly speaking, the gospel of Christ would never have taken such fast hold on the strong, practical, vigorous nations of the West had it not been for these epistles. The mind of the apostle John is given to deep and spiritual insight, which sees rather than argues its way into the truths of the gospel. The mind of the apostle Peter is specially Hebraic: Peter looks at everything from the standpoint of his early education and training, on which the teachings of his Master had been grafted. But with Paul, though he writes as a Hebrew of the Hebrews, employing methods of Scripture interpretation that are unfamiliar to our thought, yet his epistles are characterized by a virility, a logical order, a style of argument, a finiteness of statement and phraseology that are closely akin to our Western civilization. When Paul was born, the Roman Empire was in the summer of its glory and Greek culture was so infused into the universal thought and speech that even the exclusivism and bigotry of the Jewish ghettos were not wholly proof against it. The breath of the Western ocean is in these epistles; the tides of the coming centuries were already rolling into the estuary and causing the barges of long stationary tradition to move uneasily and rattle their mooring chains. It is for this reason that Paul has been the contemporary of Western civilization through all the centuries. It was he who taught Augustine and inspired Luther. His thoughts and conceptions have been wrought into the texture and woven into the woof of the foremost minds of the Christian centuries. The seeds he scattered have fruited in the harvests of modern education, jurisprudence, liberty, and civilization.

"Ah!" it has been eloquently said, "what does the world owe to this apostle? What has it owed him? What will it owe—of pious pastors, zealous missionaries, eminent Christians, useful books, benevolent endowments, examples of faith, charity, purity, holiness? Who can calculate it? The whole human race will arise and confess that among all the names of its benefactors whom it is pleased to enroll from age to age, there is no one whom it proclaims with so much harmony, gratitude, and love as the name of the apostle Paul."

We have thirteen letters bearing the inscription and signature of Paul. The evidence of their genuineness and authenticity is generally admitted. Even the extreme school of destructive criticism has been compelled to admit that the epistles to the Corinthians, Galatians, and Romans are undoubtedly Paul's. They were written under very different circumstances and at very different periods between the years A.D. 52 and 68. These when hope was young and fresh in the first glad dawn; these amid the stress of strong antagonism; these with the shackles of the prison on the wrist; these when the sun was coloring the horizon with its last intense glow. Each largely tinctured with the complexion of the worlds without and within, but all full of that devotion to the risen Lord that led him to subscribe himself so often as his devoted bondservant: Paul, a servant of Jesus Christ.

Let us place these epistles in the order of their composition and see how they mark the successive stages of progress in the apostle's conceptions of Christ. Paul was always full of love and loyalty and the divine Spirit, but according to his own words, he was perpetually leaving the things that were behind and pressing on to those before, that he might know Christ and the power of His resurrection and the fellowship of His sufferings. It is not surprising, therefore, that each of the epistles contains some profounder apprehension of the fullness and glory of the risen Lord. As Jesus is said to have increased in wisdom and stature, so His apostle was transformed into His image from glory to glory. All Paul's life was a going from strength to strength. And as Paul climbed the craggy steps of obedience and faith, of growing likeness to Jesus, of self-sacrifice and experience of the cross, his horizon of knowledge widened to tread the lengths and heights and depths of the knowledge of the love of Christ that still passed his knowledge. We have only to compare the first epistle to the Thessalonians with that of the Ephesians to perceive at once how greatly this noble nature had filled out and grown under the culture of the divine husbandman.

The best and most natural division of the epistles that I have seen is the following:

The Eschatological Group: 1 and 2 Thessalonians.
The Anti-Judaic Group: 1 and 2 Corinthians, Galatians, Romans.
The Christological or Anti-Gnostic group: Philippians, Colossians, Philemon, Ephesians.
The Pastoral Group: 1 Timothy, Titus, and 2 Timothy.

Let us consider them in this order.

1 and 2 THESSALONIANS—The first of these was probably written toward the close of the year A.D. 52, and certainly from Corinth. Timothy had been left in Macedonia to complete the work from which the apostle had been so summarily torn. After doing all he could to comfort and help the infant churches, Timothy came with Silas to Paul, and the three held solemn and prayerful conferences on the best way of directing and assisting the disciples amid the great storm of opposition through which they were passing. It was impossible for any of them to go to their relief, and so this first epistle was dispatched. And the second epistle went out from the

same city, a few months afterward, when the apostle heard that the first had been interpreted to mean that the Lord's coming was near enough to justify the expectation of the speedy dissolution of existing society.

In each of these epistles, the apostle dwells more largely than in any of the others on the second coming, whose light was illuminating his whole being with its glow. The motive for every duty, the encouragement to every Christian attitude, the ground for purity, hopefulness, comfort, and practical virtue, are found in the coming of the Son of God. "The Lord himself shall descend from heaven with a shout, with the voice of the archangel, and with the trump of God: and the dead in Christ shall rise first: Then *we* which are alive and remain shall be caught up" (1 Thess. 4:16–17).

The motive for Christian living is less in the sense of the indwelling Christ and more in the expectation of the coming Christ: there is less of the cross and more of the glory; less of the invisible headship over all things in heaven and earth, which comes out so prominently in later epistles, and more of the *parousia,* the personal presence of Jesus. To the end, the apostle bade the Church stand at her porch window, looking for the coming of the glory of her great God and Savior; but the ground covered by his later epistles is much wider than that of his earliest.

1 CORINTHIANS—Toward the end of Paul's three years' residence in Ephesus, tidings came, partly through Apollos and partly through members of the house of Chloe, of the very unfavorable condition of affairs at Corinth. Amid the strongly sensuous influences of the voluptuous city, the little band of converts seemed on the point of yielding to the strong current setting against them and relapsing into the vices of their contemporaries. Shortly after this, a letter arrived from the church itself, brought to Ephesus by Stephanas, Fortunatus, and Achaicus, asking advice on a number of practical difficulties. It was a terrible revelation of quarrels, disputings, inconsistencies, and grosser evils and was enough to daunt any man. How could Paul hope to remedy such a state of things without going in person? And if he went, how would he be received? At that time, he was pressed with the terrible conflict that was being waged at Ephesus, and he must stay at his post. There was nothing Paul could do but to write as the Holy Spirit might

direct. The result is the marvelous epistle, which more than any other has supplied practical direction to the Church in the following centuries, showing her how to apply the principles of the gospel to the most complicated moral and social problems. It was carried to Corinth by Titus. In this epistle there is still the heartbeat of the second coming, but there are, in addition, the sublime conception of the second Adam and the revelation by the Holy Spirit to spiritual minds of things that the eye had not seen, nor ear heard, nor the heart of man conceived.

2 CORINTHIANS—When the riot broke out in Ephesus, the apostle was eagerly looking for the coming of Titus with tidings of the reception of his epistle. On his expulsion from the city, Paul sent to Troas, making sure that he would meet Titus there. But failing to do so, he became feverishly anxious and hastened on to Macedonia to seek him. He was afflicted on every side: "without were fightings, within were fears" (7:5), till he was finally comforted by the coming of Titus, who brought good news as he told of their longing, their mourning, their zeal for Paul. Thereupon he wrote his second epistle and sent it to the church by the hands of Titus and another.

This is the most personal of all his epistles. Paul lays bare his heart, permitting us to see its yearning tenderness, its sensitiveness to love or hate, its eager devotion to the best interests of his converts. "All things are for your sakes.... For which cause we faint not" (4:15–16). The deep spiritual aspects of the Christian life that are so characteristic of the later epistles are specially unfolded. Paul writes as though, under the teaching of the Holy Spirit, he were enjoying increasing measures of the life hid with Christ in God. Though Paul was always delivered unto death for Jesus' sake, the life of Jesus that was in him was manifesting itself in his mortal flesh (4:11). Paul now knew Christ, not after the flesh but in the spirit; the constraint of His love was perpetually leading to the denial of self and the putting on of the new creation that was the gift of the risen Lord (5:14–17). Whatever the difficulties and privations of his circumstances, Paul was amply compensated from the eternal and spiritual sphere in which he lived (6:4–10). And though the thorn in the flesh cost him continual anguish, the grace of Jesus made him glory in it as positively a source of strength (12:9–10).

GALATIANS—Paul followed Titus to Corinth and remained there a happy three months. But the joy of fellowship with the large and happy band of friends who gathered around him there must have been greatly blurred by tidings of the fickleness of the Galatians, who were moving away "from him that called you into the grace of Christ unto another gospel" (1:6). Proselytizers had gone among his converts professing to represent the church at Jerusalem, and in the name of primitive Christianity, they had disparaged Paul's apostleship, questioned his authority, and insisted on the necessity of Gentiles being circumcised and submitting to the Levitical law.

It was a critical hour. If these views had prevailed, Christianity would have dwindled into a Jewish sect, and the river of Christian life and work that had gushed from the ground at Pentecost would have lost itself among the sands of rabbinical speculation. Gentile Christianity was in the balance, the hope of the world at stake. Profoundly stirred in spirit, the apostle's righteous indignation flames in almost every sentence, and with glowing passion he meets the arguments of those who were seducing the Galatians from the simplicity and freedom of Christ: "As we said before, so say I now again. If any man preach any other gospel unto you than that ye have received, let him be accursed" (1:9).

Under the glow of his indignation, not only is there clear and strong thinking, but there is indication of yet further regions of Christian knowledge that were being unfolded to Paul. Pressed by the urgency of his position—and how often the arising of new heresies had driven God's servants deeper into the fullness treasured up in Christ for all needs and times—Paul is led to realize that not Moses but Abraham, not Sinai but the tents of the patriarch, were the true origin of the Jewish people. Abraham was called when yet in uncircumcision; he believed and was justified by faith thirty years before he received the distinctive Jewish rite. It was as great a revelation as the shores of the New World to Columbus; and from that moment, Paul sprang up to an altogether new position, from which he was able to successfully meet the assaults of the Judaizer and vindicate all believing Gentiles as children of believing Abraham and heirs of the covenant of promise.

ROMANS—As his stay in Corinth drew to a close, the apostle's mind was attracted to the church in the world's metropolis. Paul hoped very soon to visit them, and by way of preparation for his coming, he prepared a succinct and connected view of the truths that had been revealed to his profoundest thought by the divine Spirit. Thus originated the greatest of his epistles, that to the Romans.

In this, as in the former, there is not only a clear appreciation and presentation of the great doctrine of justification by faith but also an ever-enlarging view of our identification with Christ and of His indwelling. Paul says we were *reconciled* to God by the *death* of His Son, but we are *saved* by His *life*. He speaks of reigning in life through the abundance of grace treasured up in the one Man, Jesus Christ. His words glow with rapture as he speaks of being joined to Him who was raised from the dead and of our freedom from the old bondage in which we were held. So entirely had Christ become one with him and he one with Christ that Paul felt the unutterable groans of His intercessions and something of His travail for the souls of men. Paul had yielded his members as weapons in his mighty warfare against sin, being crucified with Christ, and now no longer lived, but Christ lived in him. His life was one of faith in the Son of God, who loved him and gave Himself for him. The cross was the means not of justification only but of sanctification and stood between Paul and his past, while by the Holy Spirit, the Son of God had become resident and was reigning within him.

PHILIPPIANS—There is nothing polemical in this epistle. The former epistles have met and silenced Paul's detractors and enemies. The strife and divisions of the churches, if such there were, do not reach him through the prison doors or travel the distance to his Roman abode. The peace of God that passes all understanding keeps his mind and heart, and out of that tranquil heart pours forth a tide of deep and tender love to his beloved friends at Philippi.

The hope of being alive at the coming of the Lord is still his heart's guiding star. His citizenship was in heaven, from whence he looked for the Savior, the Lord Jesus Christ. But the possibility that perhaps the Lord might have to be magnified by his death had already presented itself to his mind. He saw, however, that the will of God was best, and he learned from his Master the secret of self-sacrificing humility. Epaphroditus had brought gifts of love from Philippi, and by his hands this letter of love and gratitude was returned.

COLOSSIANS—Among those who visited Paul in his hired house toward the end of his imprisonment in Rome was Epaphras of Colossae, who also represented Laodicea and Hierapolis—cities of Asia Minor in the valley of the Lycus. Epaphras told the apostle of a strange new heresy that was developing with alarming rapidity in the churches that had been planted in those distant cities.

The falsely called Christian philosophy of the time was endeavoring to fill the gulf between sinful man and the holy God by a ladder of mythical existences, through which man's prayers might ascend to God and His blessing descend on man. The whole conception was entirely imaginary, and at its further reach must fail of its object, for between the littlest archangel or spirit and the eternal God there is still the infinite chasm that separates the creature from the Creator and is impassable unless the Creator come across it.

The necessity of dealing with this absurd tissue of the imagination was used by the Spirit of God to unveil a wider, deeper view of the fullness that there is in Jesus; and a disclosure was made to the apostle of the full meaning of the Lord's ascension to the right hand of power. He saw that all principalities and powers, all creature existences, all beings in heaven and on earth and under the earth, were beneath His feet. He was Lord and King, ruling all, filling all, maintaining all. "For by him were all things created, that are in heaven, and that are in earth, visible and invisible, whether they be thrones, or dominions, or principalities, or powers: all things were created by him, and for him: And he is before all things, and by him all things consist.... And ye are complete in him, which is the head of all principality and power" (1:16–17; 2:10).

At the same time, Paul's conviction of his union with the risen Lord was ever more definite, and his appreciation of His indwelling more full of hope and glory. What did it matter whether he was called upon to fill up what was behind of the sufferings of Christ? Had it not been given him to make known the riches of the glory of this mystery among the Gentiles, which is Christ in the heart, the hope of glory? Tychicus bore this letter and that to the Ephesians.

PHILEMON—Onesimus, the runaway slave, fugitive from his master Philemon, driven by need to the apostle's house or discovered in some low haunt of crime by his companions in their errands of mercy, had been born again to a new life and was now not a slave only but a brother beloved. Paul sent him back to his master, who was a friend of Paul's and with whom he seems to have had a business account (v. 17–19). This epistle, the perfect model of Christian courtesy, was given Onesimus as an introduction to his owner.

The chief point to notice here is the perfect patience and certainty with which the apostle awaits the ultimate triumph of divine love. Paul must have felt that in the sight of God, Onesimus had a perfect right to freedom. But it would have been highly impolitic for him to interfere between master and man. Let Philemon be taught to look at Onesimus as joined to him in the gospel, and it would not be long before he would himself propose his emancipation. But till he did, Paul would not precipitate matters, and Onesimus must return to serve. The principle of action in this single instance doubtless became the ultimate law for the solution of many other difficult problems that were left to the gradual conquest of the spirit of love.

EPHESIANS—This epistle reiterates the great conceptions of the empire of the Lord Jesus and of His ability to fill the whole gulf between God and man which the former epistle had foreshadowed. The doctrine of identification with Christ—in His death, resurrection, and ascension—is set forth with remarkable vividness and power. The conception of the Church as the Body and Bride of Christ is elaborated with peculiar beauty of detail. But the commanding peculiarity of this epistle is its allusion to the home life of husband and wife, parent and child, master and slave.

In earlier days, on account of the present distress and without the distinct assurance of inspiration, the apostle had spoken as though the difficulties of married life outweighed its blessings (1 Cor. 7). But in these later epistles, Paul holds marriage up as the model of the love that subsists between the Heavenly Bridegroom and His own; and contrary to the opinion of his time, Paul goes so far as to assert that the true bond of marriage is the self-sacrifice of the stronger for the weaker—of the husband for the wife. Woman was no longer to be the slave or toy of man, but men were to be prepared to give themselves for their wives in loving acts of unselfishness, as Christ loved the Church and gave Himself for it.

1 TIMOTHY and TITUS—After his release, Paul visited the scenes of his former ministry around the shores of the Aegean. It

was during his journeys at this time that he wrote these epistles to direct the young evangelists in the proper ordering of the churches under their care. The letters are of extreme interest because they deal with so many domestic and practical details. Paul is never weary of showing that the principles of the gospel are meant to elevate the commoner incidents and duties of life. "Godliness is profitable unto all things, having promise of the life that now is" (1 Tim. 4:8). "For the grace of God that bringeth salvation hath appeared to all men, teaching us that, denying ungodliness and worldly lusts, we should live soberly, righteously, and godly, in this present world" (Titus 2:11–12).

2 TIMOTHY—It was a mellow and softened old age. Lonely so far as dear companions were concerned; full of privations, without cloak or books or helpers; shivering in the prison; waiting to be offered, weigh anchor, and drop down the stream. He wanted once more to see his beloved son in the faith and wrote to speed Timothy's steps. It is very moving, very beautiful, very human. But the ray of an indomitable courage and faith is flung across the heaving waters. Paul has kept his Lord's deposit and knows that the deposit that he had made years before had been no less safely kept. And so the pen is taken in hand for the last time. A few tender messages are added as a postscript. And with large letters he appends the closing sentences, "The Lord Jesus Christ be with thy spirit. Grace be with you."

The epistles of Paul resemble stereotyped plates from which innumerable copies are produced. Who but God can number the myriads of souls that have come in contact with Paul's words and have themselves become epistles, ministered by him, "written not with ink, but with the Spirit of the living God" (2 Cor. 3:3). And till the Lord come, edition after edition of character, soul life, and blessed victorious experience shall be struck off from these blocks of holy thinking that we owe to the apostle Paul.